Acclaim for
SCHEHERA~

"A savvy treatment of that ultimate piece of emotional baggage: sex. Mernissi is as bracing and intelligent as Scheherazade—and her grasp of sexual politics, both East and West, is not just piquant but spot-on."

—*Kirkus Reviews*

"Rich and informative."

—*Women's Review of Books*

"As an interpreter of Arab culture alone, Fatema Mernissi would be brilliant. But beyond that, she is that rare treasure, an original thinker—always curious, always in search of reason, and always wonderfully female."

—Mark Kurlansky, author of *The White Man in the Tree*

"In her spellbinding storyteller's voice, and with the vast erudition and clever wit for which she is famous, Mernissi swoops us up on a dazzling rummage through harems fabricated out of men's fantasies, fears, and needs to dominate. On her journey westward, this worthy daughter of Scheherazade tosses us keys to the strange world that is our own, enticing us to enter—if we dare. A tough, smart, totally mesmerizing, and deeply revealing book that will not leave you complacent."

—Margot Badran, author of *Feminists, Islam, and Nation*

"In a valiant attempt to clear up the Orientalist fabrications of harems, Mernissi provides a beguiling insider's perspective. At long last, Scheherazade regains her clothes and her intellect is once again installed."

—Alev Lytle Croutier, author of *Harem: The World Behind the Veil*

# Scheherazade Goes West

## Different Cultures, Different Harems

### Fatema Mernissi

WASHINGTON SQUARE PRESS

NEW YORK   LONDON   TORONTO   SYDNEY   SINGAPORE

Lyrics from the song "Go East, Young Man" from the motion picture soundtrack to *Harum Scarum,* courtesy of Cherry Lane Music and R&H Music.

Lyric excerpt of "Go East, Young Man" by Bernie Baum, Bill Giant and
   Florence Kaye
Copyright © 1965 by Elvis Presley Music, Inc.
Copyright Renewed and Assigned to Elvis Presley Music
   (Administered by R&H Music)
International Copyright Secured    Reprinted by Permission
All Rights Reserved

*The Misanthrope and Other Plays,* by Molière and translated by John Wood and David Coward, copyright © 1959, courtesy of Penguin Putnam, London, England.

*The Art of Love* by Ovid, translated by Rolfe Humphries, p. 46, 1957. Courtesy of Indiana University Press, Bloomington, Indiana.

A Washington Square Press Publication of
POCKET BOOKS, a division of Simon & Schuster, Inc.
1230 Avenue of the Americas, New York, NY 10020

Copyright © 2001 by Fatema Mernissi

Originally published in hardcover in 2001 by Washington Square Press

ISBN: 0-7434-1243-5

First Washington Square Press trade paperback printing March 2002

10 9 8 7 6 5 4 3 2

WASHINGTON SQUARE PRESS and colophon are
registered trademarks of Simon & Schuster, Inc.

For information regarding special discounts for bulk purchases,
please contact Simon & Schuster Special Sales at 1-800-456-6798 or
business@simonandschuster.com

Cover design by Anna Dorfman
Cover art, top: *Scheherazade,* by Hermann Emil Sprengel © Philips, The International Fine Art
Auctioneers; cover art, bottom: *Sultan in His Harem* © Archivo Iconografico, S.A./Corbis; cover
art, background: © Robert Frerck/Woodfin Camp/Picture Quest

Printed in the U.S.A.

To Professor Mohamed Chafik, my high school teacher, who taught me, through his pre-Islamic poetry class, that in our Moroccan heritage, be it Arab or Berber, dialogue-nurturing is considered magic, because it fuels power with beauty.

# Contents

# Contents

# Contents

# I

# The Tale of the Lady
# with the Feather Dress

If by chance you were to meet me at the
Casablanca airport or on a boat sailing from Tangiers, you would think me self-confident, but I am
not. Even now, at my age, I am frightened when crossing
borders because I am afraid of failing to understand
strangers. "To travel is the best way to learn and empower
yourself," said Yasmina, my grandmother, who was illiterate and lived in a harem, a traditional household with
locked gates that women were not supposed to open. "You
must focus on the strangers you meet and try to understand them. The more you understand a stranger and the
greater is your knowledge of yourself, the more power you
will have." For Yasmina, the harem was a prison, a place
women were forbidden to leave. So she glorified travel and
regarded the opportunity to cross boundaries as a sacred
privilege, the best way to shed powerlessness. And, indeed,

rumors ran wild in Fez, the medieval city of my childhood, about trained Sufi masters who got extraordinary "flashes" *(lawami')* and expanded their knowledge exponentially, simply because they were so focused on learning from the foreigners who passed through their lives.

A few years ago, I had to visit ten Western cities for the promotion of my book, *Dreams of Trespass: Tales of a Harem Girlhood,* which appeared in 1994 and was translated into twenty-two languages. During that tour, I was interviewed by more than a hundred Western journalists and I soon noticed that most of the men grinned when pronouncing the word "harem." I felt shocked by their grins. How can anyone smile when invoking a word synonymous with prison, I wondered. For my grandmother Yasmina, the harem was a cruel institution that sharply curtailed her rights, starting with the "right to travel and discover Allah's beautiful and complicated planet," as she put it. But according to Yasmina's philosophy, which I later discovered she had adopted from the Sufis, the mystics of Islam, I needed to transform my feelings of shock toward the Western journalists into an openness to learn from them. At first, I had great difficulty doing so and started wondering if perhaps, due to my age, I was losing my capacity to adapt to new situations. I felt terrified of becoming stiff and unable to digest the unexpected. No one noticed my anxiety during my book promotion tour, however, because I was wearing my huge Berber silver bracelet and my red Chanel lipstick.

To learn from travel, one must train oneself to capture messages. "You must cultivate *isti'dad,* the state of readiness," Yasmina used to whisper conspiratorially in my ear, so as to exclude those whom she regarded as unworthy of the Sufi tradition. "The most baggage carried by strangers is their difference. And if you focus on the divergent and the dissimilar, you get 'flashes.' " Then she would remind me to keep this lesson secret. "*Teqiyeh,* secrecy, is the name of the game," she would say. "Remember what happened to poor Hallaj!" Hallaj was a famous Sufi who was arrested by the Abbasid police in A.D. 915 for publicly proclaiming in the streets of Baghdad: "I am the Truth" (*Ana l'haq*). Since Truth is one of the names for God, Hallaj was declared a heretic. Islam insists on the unbridgeable distance between the divine and the human, but Hallaj believed that if you concentrate on loving God, without intermediaries, a blurring of the boundaries with the divine becomes possible. Arresting Hallaj disturbed the Abbasid police, because to arrest him—a man who declared himself made in the image of God—was to affront God himself. Nonetheless, Hallaj was burned alive in March 922, and since I have always believed that staying alive is preferable to self-immolation, I kept Yasmina's instructions regarding travel an absolute secret, and grew up so intent on realizing her dream that crossing borders still terrifies me.

Throughout my childhood, Yasmina often told me that it is normal for a woman to experience panic when crossing oceans and rivers. "When a woman decides to use her wings, she takes big risks," she would say, and then would add that, conversely, when a woman doesn't use her wings at all, it hurts her.

When Yasmina died, I was thirteen. I was supposed to cry, but I did not. "The best way to remember your grandmother," she told me on her deathbed, "is to keep alive the tradition of telling my favorite Scheherazade story—'The Lady with the Feather Dress.' " And so, I learned that story—narrated by Scheherazade, the heroine of *The Thousand and One Nights*—by heart. Its main message is that a woman should lead her life as a nomad. She should stay alert and be ready to move, even if she is loved. For, as the tale teaches, love can engulf you and become a prison.

At age nineteen, when I took the train to register at Mohamed V University in Rabat, I crossed one of the most dangerous frontiers of all my life—that separating Fez, my medieval hometown, a labyrinth-like, ninth-century religious center, from Rabat, a modern, white metropolis with wide open city gates, situated on the edge of the Atlantic Ocean. At first, I felt so terrified of Rabat, with its large avenues, that I could not even move about without Kemal, a fellow student who happened to be from my neighborhood in Fez. But Kemal kept repeating that he was confused about my feelings for him. "I wonder sometimes if you love me, or if you just need me as a buffer against the thousand other men who have flocked here from all over Morocco to register at this university," he would say. What I resented most about Kemal in those days was his incredible ability to read my mind. But one reason I became fond of him was that he knew Yasmina's tale by heart. However, his version was the official one, published in the book version of *The Thousand and One Nights* (better known to many English readers as *The Arabian Nights*). And he told me that illiterate women like Yasmina were more subversive than educated ones both because they introduced heretical distortions into the tales and because they used storytelling, that oral medium, to escape censorship. Throughout Muslim history, he said, the oral tradition has reduced even the most tyrannical of despots to powerlessness.

According to Kemal, the first distortion that Yasmina introduced into her favorite tale was to feminize its title. In the book version of *The Thousand and One Nights,* the story is called "The Tale of Hassan al Basri," Basra being a city in southern Iraq, at the crossroads between the Mediterranean and trade roads heading toward China. But the tale that I inherited from Yasmina was entitled "The Lady with the Feather Dress," and it opens in Baghdad, then the capital of the Muslim empire. From Baghdad, Hassan, a handsome but bankrupt youth who had squandered his entire fortune on wine and gallant company, sailed away to strange islands to seek his fortune. Gazing at the sea from a high terrace one night, he was struck by the graceful movements of a large bird who had alighted on the beach. Suddenly the bird shed what turned out to be a dress made of feathers, and out stepped a beautiful naked woman, who ran to swim in the waves. "She outdid in beauty all human beings. She had a mouth as magical as Solomon's seal and hair blacker than the night. . . . She had lips like corals and teeth like strung pearls. . . . Her middle was full of folds. . . . She had thighs great and plump, like marble columns." But what captivated Hassan Basri the most was what lay between her thighs: "a goodly rounded dome on pillars borne, like a bowl of silver or crystal."[1]

Smitten with love, Hassan stole the beauty's feather dress while she was swimming and buried it in a secret tomb. Deprived of her wings, the woman became his captive. Hassan married her, showered her with silks and precious stones, and when she bore him two sons, relaxed his attentive tenderness, believing that she would never again think about flying. He started traveling on long trips to increase his fortune, and was astonished to discover one day when he returned that his wife, who had never stopped looking for her feather dress, had finally found it and flown away. "Taking her sons in her bosom, she wrapped herself in the feather dress and became a bird, by the ordinance of Allah to whom belongs might and majesty. Then, she walked with a swaying and graceful gait and danced and sported and flapped her wings . . . ,"[2] flying away over deep rivers and turbulent oceans to reach her native island of Wak Wak. Yet before leaving, she left a message for Hassan: He could join her if he had the courage to do so. But no one knew then, and still less knows now, where the mysterious "Wak Wak"—land of exoticism and faraway strangeness—is located. Arab historians such as Mas'udi, the ninth-century author of *Golden Meadows,* situated it in East Africa, beyond Zanzibar, while Marco Polo describes Wak Wak as the land of the Amazons, or the "female island" of Socotra. Others identify Wak Wak as being the Seychelles, Madagascar, or Malacca, and still others situate it in China or Indonesia (Java).[3]

Yasmina's second subversive distortion, according to Kemal, was her unhappy ending. In my grandmother's story, Hassan keeps desperately searching for the mysterious Wak Wak, but is never able to locate it, or to win back his wife and children. But in the book version of *The Thousand and One Nights,* recorded by men, Hassan does manage to find his wife and sons, and brings them back to Baghdad to live happily ever after. Kemal told me that men are irresistibly attracted to independent women and fall deeply in love with them, but are always terrified of being abandoned—which was why he himself resented Yasmina's ending. "To end the story the way your rebellious grandmother did, by insisting on women's privilege to abandon husbands who go on long business trips, does not help Muslim families to become stable, does it?" he said. Attacking Yasmina and blaming her for Hassan's family problems became Kemal's favorite way of expressing his jealousy whenever I wanted to respond to an invitation as an unaccompanied woman or undertake a trip by myself. He kept telling me that he wished we were still living in medieval Baghdad, where men could imprison women in harems. "Why do you think our Muslim ancestors built walled palaces with internal gardens to imprison women?" he would ask me. "Only desperately fragile men who are convinced that women have wings could create such a drastic thing as the harem, a prison that presents itself as a palace."

Every time this conversation arose, as it did too often for my taste, I tried to calm down Kemal by reminding him that men in the Christian West did not lock up women in harems. But instead of soothing him, this argument only made him flare up even more. "I do not know what goes on in the minds of Western men," he would say. "All I can tell you is that they would have built harems, too, if they saw women as an uncontrollable force. Could it be that in their fantasies, Westerners imagine women without wings? Who knows?"

The passionate debates provoked by "The Lady with the Feather Dress" went on between Kemal and myself throughout our student years, and even continued after we had become adults and started teaching at that same university, Mohamed V. Although we specialized in different fields—Kemal in medieval Arab literature and I in sociology—understanding the power of the oral tradition became important to both of us—a strategic tool with which to understand the dynamics of the modern Arab world. We rediscovered the power of our mothers' story-telling while listening to our students, who in the 1970s came mostly from the shantytowns of Casablanca and Rabat—areas not equipped with either electricity or tele-vision. If the mothers of our middle- and upper-class stu-dents had lost their power to tell stories and saw their kids fall prey to Hollywood fantasies, this was not the case for the less fortunate majority. Encouraging my sociology students to gather oral tales from the remote Atlas moun-tains and the Sahara desert, and asking literature experts to help decode them, created new occasions for Kemal and myself to collaborate—i.e., constantly contradict each other. Until, that is, we stumbled on *lawami'*, the intrigu-ing Sufi "flashes" that so often turned up in our heated ac-ademic debates. And what puzzled both of us and our students the most was that in many oral tales, the cleverer sex is rarely the one that religious authorities would ex-pect. If Muslim laws give men the right to dominate women, the opposite seems to be true in the oral tradi-tion.

Never were Kemal and our passionate conversations so present in my mind as when I had to face the inquisitive stares of the Western journalists I met while on my memo-rable book promotion tour. What the journalists could not even begin to suspect was how fragile I felt behind my makeup and heavy silver jewelry. And one major reason that I felt so fragile, I soon discovered, was that I knew hardly anything about Westerners and even less so about their fantasies.

---

1. The English translation used here is that of Richard F. Burton, *The Book of the 1001 Nights and a Night* (London: Burton Club For Private Subscribers, 1886), vol. VIII, p. 33. The Arabic original used here is "Hikayat alf lila wa lila," al Maktaba ach-cha'biya, Beyrouth, Lebanon, vol. III, p. 383.

2. Ibid., p. 59.

3. Ibid., p. 61.

# 2

# Sex in the Western Harem

I never realized until my book tour that a smile can betray so much of one's inner feelings. Arabs, like many Westerners, think it is the eyes that give one away. "The eye is the wide gateway to the soul," wrote Ibn Hazm, an expert on love, "the scrutinizer of its secrets, conveying its most private thoughts."[1] Growing up, I was taught that a woman should lower her gaze, so that men could never know her thoughts. The so-called modesty of Arab women is in fact a war tactic. But the smile, I discovered during my book tour, can give one away as easily as the eye—and in many different ways. Not all of those journalists' smiles were alike. Each, according to nationality, expressed a different mixture of feelings.

We can break the West into two camps as far as smiles are concerned: the Americans and the Europeans. The American men, upon hearing the word "harem," smiled with unadulterated and straightforward embarrassment. Whatever the word means for Americans hinges on something linked to shame. The Europeans, in contrast, responded with smiles that varied from polite reserve in the North to merry exuberance in the South, with subtleties fluctuating according to the distance of the journalists' origin from the Mediterranean. French, Spanish, and Italian men had a flirtatious, amused light in their eyes. Scandinavians and Germans, with the exception of the Danes, had astonishment in theirs—astonishment tinged with shock. "Were you really born in a harem?" they would ask, looking intently at me with a mixture of apprehension and puzzlement.

My book starts with the sentence: "I was born in a harem," and that short sentence seemed to contain some mysterious problem, because everyone, without exception, started his interview by asking, like a magic formula, "So, were you really born in a harem?" The intensity of the look accompanying the inquiry signaled that my interviewer did not want me to evade the question—as if there were some shameful secret involved. Yet for me, not only is the word "harem" a synonym for the family as an institution, but it would also never occur to me to associate it with something jovial. After all, the very origin of the Arabic word "haram," from which the word "harem" is derived, literally refers to sin, the dangerous frontier where sacred law and pleasure collide. *Haram* is what the religious law forbids;

the opposite is *halal*, that which is permissible. But evidently, when crossing the frontier to the West, the Arabic word "harem" lost its dangerous edge. Why else would Westerners associate it with euphoria, with the absence of constraints? In their harem, sex is anxiety-free.

Suddenly, during these book interviews, I felt trapped in a strangely solemn and dramatic situation totally out of place in the usual mundane world of book promotion tours. I felt that if I said, "Yes, I was born in a harem," I would immediately create a problem for both my interviewers and myself. Why is this happening? I kept wondering. My feminine intuition, which starts functioning at full speed when strange things occur, was alerting me to the fact that these smiles had sexual undertones that I couldn't read. The journalists were perceiving a "harem" that was invisible to me.

I called Christiane, my French editor in Paris, for a Western woman's perspective.

"Sure, their smiles have to do with sex," she said, and then added, "Why don't you push them to be more talkative?"

That is when I decided to reverse roles by interviewing the male journalists who were interviewing me. "Why are you smiling?" I would ask softly when yet another one exhibited signs of excitement. "What is amusing about the harem?" This two-way exchange turned my ex-interviewers into helpful informants who soon taught me that we were not talking about the same thing: Westerners had their harem and I had mine, and the two had nothing in common.

Apparently, the Westerner's harem was an orgiastic feast where men benefited from a true miracle: receiving sexual pleasure without resistance or trouble from the women they had reduced to slaves. In Muslim harems, men expect their enslaved women to fight back ferociously and abort their schemes for pleasure. The Westerners also referred primarily to pictorial images of harems, such as those seen in paintings or films, while I visualized actual palaces—harems built of high walls and real stones by powerful men such as caliphs, sultans, and rich merchants. My harem was associated with a historical reality. Theirs was associated with artistic images created by famous painters such as Ingres, Matisse, Delacroix, or Picasso—who reduced women to odalisques (a Turkish word for a female slave)—or by talented Hollywood movie-makers, who portrayed harem women as scantily clad belly-dancers happy to serve their captors. Some journalists also mentioned operas like Verdi's *Aida* or ballets like Diaghilev's *Scheherazade*. But whatever image they referred to, the journalists always described the harem as a voluptuous wonder-land drenched with heavy sex provided by vulnerable nude women who were happy to be locked up.

This is indeed a miracle, I thought as I listened to the Westerners' descriptions. Muslim male artists are much more realistic when it comes to envisioning the harem as a source of erotic bliss. Even in their fantasies, as expressed in

miniature paintings or in legends and literature, Muslim ⌉
men expect women to be highly aware of the inequality in- |
herent in the harem system and therefore unlikely to en- ⌋
thusiastically satisfy their captors' desires.

Many of the Muslim courts employed artists who illustrated art books with miniature paintings. The paintings
were not hung on walls, or exhibited in museums, but were
kept as a private luxury, to be enjoyed only by the rich and
the powerful, who could contemplate them whenever they
liked. Contrary to what many Westerners believe, Islam has
a rich tradition of secular painting, in spite of its ban on images. It is only in religious rituals that the use of pictorial representation is totally prohibited. From the eighth century
onward, Muslim dynasties invested consistently in secular
painting. The Umayyad princes decorated their pleasure
house of Qusayr 'Amra (in what is now the Transjordan
desert, near the Dead Sea) with huge frescoes, while the
sixteenth-century Safavid dynasty of Persia raised the art of
miniature painting to its highest peak. Most of the miniatures
illustrated legends and love poems, and were thus an opportunity for both writers and painters to express their fantasies
about women, love, passion—and the risks involved therein.
⌈In both miniatures and literature, Muslim men represent
women as active participants,⌋ while Westerners such as Matisse, Ingres, and Picasso show them as nude and passive.
Muslim painters imagine harem women as riding fast
horses, armed with bows and arrows, and dressed in heavy

coats. Muslim men portray harem women as uncontrollable sexual partners. But Westerners, I have come to realize, see the harem as a peaceful pleasure-garden where omnipotent men reign supreme over obedient women. While Muslim men describe themselves as insecure in their harems, real or imagined, Westerners describe themselves as self-assured heroes with no fears of women. The tragic dimension so present in Muslim harems—fear of women and male self-doubt—is missing in the Western harem.

The most talkative of the male journalists I met during my book tour were the Mediterranean Europeans. They would define the harem, with sly laughter full of malice, as "a wonderful place where beautiful women are sexually available." Many sophisticated Frenchmen, on the other hand, associated the harem with paintings depicting brothels, like those by Henri de Toulouse-Lautrec (*Au Salon de la rue des Moulins,* 1894) and Edgar Degas (*The Client,* 1879). Most of the Scandinavians just blushed and smiled at the mere mention of the "forbidden" word, letting me infer that politeness and good manners require that some embarrassing subjects best be avoided. The exception to this rule were the Danes, who behaved more like their French and Spanish colleagues by bursting into merry laughter at first, and then, when slightly encouraged, going into great detail about the luxurious embroidered silks that the harem women wear, their long and uncombed hair, and their supine, patiently waiting positions.

Many American journalists described the harem women as Hollywood-inspired dancing slaves. One even started whistling the song that Elvis Presley, dressed as an Arab, performed when he invaded a harem to rescue a sequestered beauty in *Harum Scarum* (1965):

I am gonna go where the desert sun is, where the
    fun is;
go where the harem girls dance;
go where there's love and romance . . .
To say the least, go East, young men.
You'll feel like the Sheik, so rich and grand, with
    dancing girls at your command.
When paradise starts calling, into some tent I'm
    crawling.
I'll make love the way I plan. Go East
and drink and feast.
Go East, young men.[2]

Jim, a Paris-based American journalist who earns his living by writing about films, taught me a Hollywood expression regarding sexy Oriental movies that I had never heard before: "t and s." The letter "t" stands for "tits" and the letter "s" for "sand."[3] As we were talking, the Disney version of *Aladdin*, which appeared in 1992 shortly after the Gulf War ended, came up, and another journalist hummed the opening song of the movie.[4]

Other Americans remembered the 1917 and 1918 Twentieth Century Fox screen versions of *Aladdin and His Lamp*
and *Ali Baba and the Forty Thieves,* or the 1920 *Kismet,* while
the multiple versions of *The Thief of Baghdad* seemed to be a
cultural landmark of sorts in Western men's psyche. Some
quoted the 1924 Douglas Fairbanks version, others the 1940
version, and still others, the 1961 French-Italian version starring Steve Reeves. The 1978 television version, where the
caliph of Baghdad was none other than Peter Ustinov, was
also mentioned. And an elderly journalist quoted *The Sheik*
(1921) with Rudolph Valentino while smiling and caressing
an imaginary mustache.

When I envision a harem, I think of a densely populated
place where everyone is always watching everyone else. In
Muslim harems, even married men and women have great
difficulty finding a private place in which to caress each
other. As for the married women in the harem, sexual grat-
ification is impossible since they must share their men with
hundreds of frustrated "colleagues." So when you think
calmly about what a harem is, pornographic bliss is a totally
unrealistic expectation. Even if a man kills himself at the
task and stuffs himself full with aphrodisiacs, which were
an important component of the harem culture, court
chronicles reveal that even the most entranced of lovers
could outdo himself only sometimes, and then only with
that single woman he adored, for as long as his flame kept
burning. Meanwhile, the other wives and concubines had

to live with their frustrations. So how, I wondered, did Western men create their images of an idyllic, lustful harem?

In Western images of harems, women have no wings, no horses, and no arrows. These Western harems, unlike Muslim ones, are not about terrible sex-wars during which women resist, disturb men's schemes, and sometimes become masters, confusing caliphs and emperors alike. One of the women most often portrayed in Muslim miniatures—be they Persian, Turkish, or Mughal—is Zuleikha, from the biblical legend of Joseph, as narrated in Sura 12 (Verse 12) of the Koran under the title "Yusuf." The story unfolds in Egypt, where Zuleikha, a mature woman married to a powerful man, Putiphar, falls madly in love with the handsome Yusuf when her husband brings him home, expecting her to adopt him as a son. The miniatures show her as an aggressive female sexually harassing the pious Yusuf, who miraculously resists her seductive moves, thus maintaining law and order. The miniatures echo the tragic potentiality of adultery, especially when initiated by a sexually frustrated married woman. However, although the Koran narrates the main events of the legend, Muslim artists do not refer, strangely enough, to the sacred text as the source of their inspiration. Instead, they claim the two giant Persian poets, Firdawsi and Jami, who both wrote a "Yusuf and Zuleikha" epic, the first around A.D. 1010, and the second around 1483.⁵ And, although the sacred and profane sources have strikingly different endings, both share one single feature: Zuleikha's capacity to neutralize law and instate chaos.[6]

But to get back to the texts. Although I myself cannot, unfortunately, read either Firdawsi or Jami in the original, being illiterate in Persian, I am always bewitched whenever I read Sura 12 of the Koran, so powerful is its poetry. Sura 12 describes Yusuf as a handsome young man who is a victim of sexual harassment: "And she, in whose house he was, asked of him an evil act. She bolted the doors and said: Come. He said: I seek refuge in Allah!" (Sura 12:23).[7] The Arabic expression used in the verse, *"rawadathu 'an Nafsih,"* is quite explicit: It literally means that she harassed him sexually.

The Sura of Yusuf starts with suspense, in which the reader is invited to help solve a riddle: Who attacked whom? Was it Zuleikha who physically assaulted the pious Yusuf, whose shirt was torn to pieces (12:26), or was it Yusuf who attacked Zuleikha? No wonder the legend is so obsessively reproduced by Muslim artists—its topic is not so much adultery as its probability. Men can make marriage laws and declare them sacred, but there is always a possibility that women will not feel bound by them. And it is this small chance that women might not obey and thereby destabilize the male order that is so striking a component of Muslim culture in both historical reality and fantasy.

As one might expect, Zuleikha, the adulteress, is denied the privilege of having her name in the Koran; she is referred to only as "she." There is also a sect, the extremist "Ajarida," that refuses to admit that the Sura of Yusuf is part of the Koran. According to Shahrastani, a Persian writer of the twelfth century, the Ajarida claim that "A love story cannot be part of the Koran."[8] This might sound logical, if love is considered to be a threat to the established order, but it is the logic of extremism, not of Islam. And this distinction is crucial if we are to understand what is going on in the Muslim world today. Yes, there are Muslim extremists who kill women in the streets of Afghanistan and Algeria, but it is because they are extremists, not because they are Muslim. These same extremists also kill male journalists who insist on expressing different opinions and introducing pluralism into the political dynamic. Islam, both as a legal and a cultural system, is imbued with the idea that the feminine is an uncontrollable power—and therefore the unknowable "other." All the passionate if not hysterical debates about women's rights taking place today in Muslim parliaments from Indonesia to Dakar are in actuality debates about pluralism. These debates relentlessly focus on women because women represent the stranger within the *Umma,* the Muslim community. It is no wonder that the first decision of Imam Khomeini, who paradoxically declared Iran a republic in 1979, was to ask women to veil. Elections, yes. Pluralism, no. The Imam knew what he was doing. He knew that an unveiled woman forces the Imam to face the fact that the *Umma,* the community of believers, is not homogeneous.

In Islamic societies, politicians can manipulate almost everything. But thus far, no fundamentalist leader has been able to convince his supporters to renounce Islam's central virtue—the principle of strict equality between human beings, regardless of sex, race, or creed. Women, like Christians or Jews, are considered to be the equal of men in Islam, even though they are granted a minority status that restricts their legal rights and denies them access to the decision-making process. Women in most Islamic nations can participate in their countries' respective decision-making bodies, but only indirectly. Women have a legal status similar to the *dhimmi* ("protected") status of religious minorities and are represented in parliament by a *wali* or *wakil.* Since the *wali* or *wakil* (literally, "representative") is necessarily a Muslim male, women and minorities are condemned to invisibility to keep the fiction of homogeneity alive.

To understand the dynamics in the Muslim world today, one has to remember that no one contests the principle of equality, which is considered to be a divine precept. What is debated is whether *Shari'a,* the law inspired by the Koran, can or cannot be changed. The debate is therefore reduced to "who" made the law. If it is men who made it, then the text can be reinterpreted; reform is possible. But extremists who oppose the democratization of the laws claim that *Shari'a* is as divine as the Koran and therefore un-changeable. The scandalous trial of the Egyptian Abu Zeid, an expert in the historicity of the Koran, who was sen-tenced as a heretic by a fundamentalist judge in an Egyp-tian court in August 1996, is but one such dramatization of this clash between the pro-democracy Ijtihad camp (*Shari'a* can be reformed because it is man-made) and the extrem-ists who oppose it.

Once again, women are the focus of this debate because sexual inequality is rooted in *Shari'a,* but even the most fer-vent extremists never argue that women are inferior, and Muslim women are raised with a strong sense of equality. This could explain why women have emerged, in spite of extremism, as political leaders in many Muslim countries, from Benazir Bhutto in Pakistan and Tançu Shiller in Turkey, to Megawati in Indonesia. It could also explain why Muslim women have aggressively infiltrated many university faculties and professional fields thought of as masculine—such as engineering—in spite of their very re-cent access to education. In the 1990s, the percentage of women teaching in universities or equivalent institutions in Egypt was higher than in either France or Canada.[9] The percentage of female students enrolled in engineering courses in Turkey and Syria was twice as high as in the United Kingdom or the Netherlands.[10] The percentage of women enrolled in engineering courses in Algeria and Egypt was higher than in Canada or Spain.[11]

One can easily predict that women will stir even more violent debates in the decade to come, as globalization forces both Muslim states and their citizens to redefine themselves and create new cultural identities, rooted more in economics than in religion. The fear of the feminine represents the threat from within; the debate about globalization, the threat from without; and both discussions will necessarily be focused on women. Femininity is the emotional locus of all kinds of disruptive forces, in both the real world and in fantasy. And, to get back to my book tour, it is this apparent absence of the feminine as a threat in the Western harem that fascinated me.

Exploring this enigmatic puzzle soon became my pleasurable obsession—pleasurable because, in the end, learning from travel and from talking to strangers did turn out to be the wonderful, enlightening experience that the Sufis and Yasmina had promised me it would be. For a university professor such as myself, who spends most of her days in either deadly silent libraries or in desperately slow Internet searches, talking to foreigners in comfortable Western cafés or lavish art bookstores was a thrilling privilege. And the secret to gaining enlightenment, I soon discovered, was to increase one's listening capacity. Where to start? Well, by shedding your arrogance, or at least trying to, and by respecting the other. Respecting a Westerner is a heroic achievement for a Muslim, a tour de force, because Western culture is so aggressively present in our daily life that we have the impression we already know it thoroughly. But in fact, as my vulnerability when facing the Western journalists made me realize, we Muslims know very little about Westerners as human beings, as bundles of contradictory hopes and yearning, unfulfilled dreams. If we could see Westerners as vulnerable, we would feel closer to them. But we confuse Westerners with Superman, with heartless, robotlike NASA architects who invest all their emotions in crafting inhuman, exorbitantly expensive spaceships to discover faraway galaxies, while neglecting their own planet. I was stunned to realize that a Western man's smile could destabilize me because I had already decided that he was a potential enemy. I had skinned him of his humanism. All my Sufi heritage, I was shocked to discover, did not protect me against the most obvious form of barbarism: the lack of respect for the foreigner. Which is, I suppose, why this book became so enriching and therapeutic for me in the end, despite many ups and downs.

My obsessive inquiry into the nature of the Western harem gave me the chance to deepen my relationships with old Western friends and to make new ones. Two journalists especially—Berlin-based Hans D. and Paris-based Jacques Dupont—became friends, so generous were they in providing me with pertinent books, key visuals, and valuable comments, all of which helped me grasp the power of the feminine as a barrier between East and West. Hans D. helped me with the thoroughness of a German tutor when he commented on the *Scheherazade* ballet that he had invited me to see, and made me understand that women's obsequiousness, their readiness to obey, is a distinctive feature of the Western harem fantasy. Jacques, on the other hand, highlighted with the humor and self-mockery that is so unique to Parisians something that is frightening to admit in serious conversation today: What attracts him to a woman, at least at the level of fantasy, is the absence of intellectual exchange. Through his comments, he clarified for me the second distinctive feature of the Western harem: Intellectual exchange with women is an obstacle to erotic pleasure. Yet in real or imagined Muslim harems, cerebral confrontation with women is necessary to achieve orgasm. Could it be that things are so different in the West? I wondered. Could it be that cultures manage emotions differently when it comes to structuring erotic responses? I was so baffled by these strange discoveries that I started with the basics: searching through dictionaries in both cultures, checking elementary words such as "odalisque," "desire," "beauty," "attraction," "sexual pleasure," and so on, and listening carefully to what the Western men had to say.

---

1. Ibn Hazm, *The Ring of the Dove: A Treatise on the Art and Practice of Arab Love*, English translation by A. J. Arberry (London: Luzac & Company, LTD, 1953), p. 34. For the purist who wants to read the Arab original, and it is worth it since the translation is regarded as blasphemous, see *Tawq al Hamama: Fi al-Alfa wa l-Ullaf*, Faroq Sa'd, ed. (Beirut: Manchourat Maktabat al Hayat, 1972), p. 70.

2. To learn more about this song, read Ella Shohat, "Gender and Culture of Empire: Toward a Feminist Ethnography of the Cinema," in *Visions of the East:*

*Orientalism in Films,* Matthew Bernstein and Gaylyn Studlar, eds. (Rutgers, N.J.: Rutgers University Press, 1997), p. 48.

3. For more information on "t" and "s," see ibid., p. 11.

4. I later learned, reading Matthew Bernstein's introduction to *Visions of the East,* that this song was the object of great controversy between the Disney Company and the American Arab Antidiscrimination Committee. The Committee attacked Disney for racist stereotyping and won the case. Disney was forced to change the lyrics that went, "I come from a land, a faraway place, where they cut off your ear, if they don't like your face." See Bernstein, op. cit., p. 17, note 20.

5. Sir Thomas Arnold, *Painting in Islam: A Study of Pictorial Art in Muslim Culture* (New York: Dover Publications, 1965), p. 106.

6. In the sacred sources, be they the Bible or the Koran, Zuleikha is depicted as a loser since Yusuf defeats her adulterous scheme by resisting her seductive moves. But the Persian poets give a happier ending to their "Zuleikha and Yusuf" stories. In their version, the prophet Yusuf, after rejecting Zuleikha in his youth, meets her again later, but hardly recognizes her, as she has grown old, ugly, sick, and destitute. Then, miraculously, he restores her beauty and health—a scene often depicted in miniatures. "The poets carried the story far beyond the point reached in the Book of Genesis or in the Quran," explains Sir Thomas Arnold in *Painting in Islam.* "Potiphar dies and Zulaykha is reduced to a state of abject poverty, and with hair turned white through sorrow, and eyes blinded by continual weeping, she dwells in a hut of reeds by the roadside, and her only solace in her misery is listening to the sound of Joseph's cavalcade as from time to time it rides past." One day, Joseph recognizes Zuleikha and "He then prays to God on her behalf, and her sight and her beauty are restored to her." Ibid., p. 108.

7. Quotation from *The Meaning of the Glorious Koran,* translated by Mohammed Marmaduke Pickthall (New York: Mentor Books, n.d.), p. 177.

8. In Arabic, "wa qalu: la yajuz an takuna qiçata l'ichqi mina l'qur'an" ("And they said: It is impossible that a love story can be part of the Koran"). From Shahrastani, *Al Milal wa-Nihal* (Beirut: dar Ça'b, 1986), vol. 1, p. 128. The author died in the year 547 of the Hijira (twelfth century). A good translation of this book is the French one by Claude Vadet, *Les Dissidences en Islam* (Paris: Geuthner, 1984). The Ajaridite position on Joseph is on page 236.

9. According to the 1996 Unesco Statistical Yearbook, the percentage of women teaching in universities or equivalent institutions is 30% in Egypt, 28% in France, and 22% in Canada.

10. According to the 1996 Unesco Statistical Yearbook, the percentage of women enrolled at the third level of engineering in universities or equivalent

institutions is 17% in Turkey (13,941 women out of a total of 81,176 students) and 17% in Syria (6,670 women out of a total of 38,675). In the Netherlands, the percentage of female students in third-level engineering is 8.4% (1,896 women out of a total of 22,475) and in the United Kingdom, 7.7% (12,261 females out of a total of 159,041).

11. According to the 1996 Unesco Statistical Yearbook, the percentage of women enrolled in engineering in Algeria and Egypt is 11.7% and 12.7% respectively, while only 9.65% in Canada and 10.66% in Spain.

# 3

# On the Western Harem Front

You would not believe how excited I get when strolling through a German bookstore, where you are free to open the books, and even sit and read comfortably on stools discreetly placed in corners for that purpose. In Rabat, a bookstore owner might throw you out if you dared to touch any of his displayed publications: You are supposed to buy the book before enjoying the sensuous pleasure of opening it. In a country where bargaining and touching goods are an integral part of the buying game, books are probably the only items that escape these traditional rituals. You can't touch the books and you can't negotiate the prices, which explains the extraordinary pleasure I have in Western bookstores, and why I dream of creating the first Rabat *Café mit Buchhandlung* (bookstore / café).

Excitement reached its peak for me in Berlin one memorable afternoon when Hans D. allowed me a glimpse of his personal harem, by looking up his favorite authors in one of that noisy city's miraculously quiet spots: the Savigny Platz art bookstore. The first book he selected was *Scènes Orientales,* where nude contemporary women posed before the camera of a male photographer in carefully choreographed harem scenes that imitated famous paintings such as Ingres's *Turkish Bath* (1862).[1] What most surprised me, as someone from the Third World, was the price of the book—about $30. "Are there enough buyers for such an expensive book?" I asked Hans, shocked, and he nodded. "Of course." The author had a French-sounding name (Alexander Dupouy), the publisher was German, the date of publication was recent (1998), and the text was in both French and German. "Europeans may disagree about elemental things such as beef and chickens," commented Hans wryly, "but our harem fantasy contributes greatly to our unification." I couldn't help laughing out loud at that, but then immediately felt embarrassed when the other bookstore customers turned around to see me holding a huge, pornographic book. I only relaxed when I remembered that I was in Savigny Platz, nearly 2,000 miles away from Rabat. Relieved, I put the book back and dutifully followed my teacher, who had by now moved on to the architecture section.

Using a ladder, Hans brought down from the top shelf a book from the 1930s entitled *The Harem: An Account of the In-*

*stitution as It Existed in the Palaces of the Turkish Sultans* by N. M. Penzer. According to Hans, the book's opening paragraph is still a valid definition of what Westerners think of when they envision a harem. "From early childhood," writes Penzer, "we have heard of the Turkish harem and have been told that it is a place where hundreds of lovely women are kept locked up for the sole pleasure of a single master. And as we grow up but little is added to this early information. . . . Most of us still imagine that the Sultan is— or, rather was—a vicious old reprobate, spending all his time in the harem, surrounded by hundreds of semi-naked women, in an atmosphere of heavy perfume, cool fountains, soft music, and over-indulgence in every conceivable kind of vice that the united brains of jealous, sex-starved women could invent for the pleasure of their lord."[2]

What shocked me when I read this paragraph was that Penzer was not afraid of the harem women's jealousy, even though he explicitly described them as being sex-starved. Only if his women were denied brains and the capacity to analyze their situation, I thought, could jealousy function as an incentive and actually increase women's desire to please men. Because when women are granted brains, trouble is sure to erupt. Sex-starved women with brains killed their masters in many Muslim harems because they understood that the competition was unfair, that it was artificially arranged. Favorite wives and concubines suffocated or poisoned caliphs out of jealousy. Caliph al-Mahdi, the founder of the Abbasid dynasty, is one famous victim of harem jealousy, poisoned one lovely August afternoon in A.D. 785 by one of his favorite women who was madly in love with him. A major problem that the harem master faces is the total transparency of his emotional state; everyone always knows who is his favorite woman of the moment. That favorite tries to hang on to her status by carefully observing her master's every move, and often notices before he does when his attention starts to shift toward a new rival. In the case of Caliph al-Mahdi, the favorite explained later when mourning over his corpse, the poisoned meal had actually been intended for her rival. "I wanted to keep you for me alone," cried the bereaved woman.[3]

When I asked Hans about this aspect of jealousy, which seemed to me extremely important, I discovered that not only did he completely agree with Penzer, but he even suggested that my position was suspect.

"Maybe your caliph had a problem, maybe he had paranoid tendencies," he said, smiling and raising his fists like a boxer in an imaginary ring. "Fatema, since we are embarking on a scientific comparison of men's psychic differences in our respective cultures, we ought to consider the possibility that Western men are less afraid of women than are Muslim men."

I asked Hans to please not attack my caliphs and indulge in sarcasm, because that's what men do everywhere, harem or no harem, to avoid getting into a serious discussion. Generously, he agreed and came to my rescue by reminding me that he was taking the "harem probe" seriously, and had put our names down on a waiting list to see the very popular *Scheherazade* ballet, originally choreographed by Sergey Diaghilev. Meanwhile, Hans said, I had to do some homework. What about making a list, he suggested, of the words used by Turks and Arabs when describing a harem woman? Intrigued by the idea, I promised to look up definitions associated with the harem so as to see whether, at least at the level of terminology, we could stumble on some enlightening differences between our cultures. I figured I could easily browse through a few dictionaries while comfortably seated in another Berlin bookstore, Arabisches Buch, and confidently promised that I would be ready with my definitions before the ballet.

But just before leaving the Savigny Platz, Hans rushed to the back of the store as if remembering something at the last minute, and, after a few words with the young man at the information desk, disappeared into the bookcases. A moment later, he was back, triumphantly waving a glossy volume like a flag. The book had a gaudy blue cover on which sprawled a huge nude woman endowed with massive buttocks and Medusa-like black hair that swirled around her distended bosom. I spotted two of the few German words I knew, *"Arabischen Nachten,"* in the subtitle.[4] What does *"Geschlechter Lust und List in den Arabischen*

*Nachten"* mean? I asked Hans in a low voice, so that no one else would hear. "Sexual desire and voluptuousness in the Arabian Nights" was his instantaneous translation. The book was a recent edition (1985) of Scheherazade's tales, illustrated by an East German artist. Yet his rendition of the Muslim storyteller was totally unfamiliar to me. I would never think of Scheherazade as nude and plump. Even though the climate is temperate in the Arab world, only delusional women in mental asylums discard their clothes. And as for plumpness, I associate it with a relaxed vision of the world. I put on weight when I am happy and lose it when I get in trouble. For my generation, who grew up on the oral tradition of storytelling, before television, heroines lose weight only when they worry. To be plump is a sign that a woman is in control of her fate.

So to my mind, Scheherazade must be thin. She has a violent husband, she is in fear of her life; I imagine her tense and strained. And what happened to Scheherazade's political messages, I wondered, before putting the book back on the shelf. Maybe the artist had a deficient copy of *The Thousand and One Nights?* But when I shared my thoughts with Hans, he gave me a lecture about democracy and pluralism.

"Maybe the German artist did have the same copy that you're familiar with," he said, "but read a different message. What about the right to freedom of thought, interpretation, and expression?" Once again, Hans seemed to be cleverer, more modern, and more democratic than me. Poor Scheherazade must be turning in her tomb and cursing me, I thought to myself—I am doing so poorly compared to men when it comes to wit and intellectual agility. It is at moments like these, when my self-esteem starts to wane, that I fall back on my Sufi streak and remind myself that to learn from foreigners, you need to go through bouts of humility. How disagreeable it is to be humble! But on that day, I did not have to go through my self-flagellation for long, because Hans looked at his watch, as Westerners so often do, and abruptly announced that he had to hurry. I hate it when Westerners look at their watch right when I am about to share an important philosophical discovery with them. And they always seem to be doing so, thus increasing the value of their own time and depreciating mine. I am forever telling myself that next time *I* will surprise *them* by interrupting them in mid-sentence, and saying with an important air, while gesturing at my watch, "I have to run." But I never seem to have the discipline to do this in a timely fashion. Oh, well, I said to myself, coming back to my Sufi heritage, as long as you learn something, feeling unappreciated is part of the deal.

Of course, as it turned out, there was no time to go through the list of harem-related words and definitions that I painstakingly prepared later that afternoon to impress Hans. When we met in front of the theater where *Scheherazade* was running, we had to stand in a long line to get in, and I soon saw that, unlike in Rabat, people don't carry on conversations in queues in Berlin. Silence is more becoming. I was shivering with the cold, but I tried to summarize my findings anyway, in order to gauge Hans's reactions and learn something about his inner thoughts. Unfortunately, we were not standing face to face, so that I could scrutinize him carefully, but side by side. But I had no choice. So I started bravely with "odalisque."

"Odalisque" is the word most commonly used in the West for a harem slave. It is a Turkish word, and has a spatial connotation, as it comes from the word *oda,* which means "room." "Literally," explains Alev Lytle Croutier, a Turkish author born in a house that had previously been occupied by the harem of a pasha, "Odalisque means 'the woman of the room,' implying a general status of servant."[5] Servant is also the meaning of *jarya,* the Arab word used for a harem slave. But while both literally mean the same thing, there is an important linguistic difference. While *odalisque* refers to a space, *jarya* refers to an activity. "*Jarya* means servant (*khadim*). . . . It comes from '*Jariy,*' to run. *Jarya* is a person at the service of someone else. She is attentive to the master's wishes and runs to grant them."[6] When I uttered the words "master's wishes," Hans nodded approvingly and remarked triumphantly that he now much preferred *jarya* to *odalisque.* In fact, he said, he would be happy to lead a media campaign to convince Europeans to switch to the Arabic word.

Female slaves, be they Arab *jarya* or Turkish *odalisques,* were either bought in slave markets or captured as booty after battles and wars. Self-education and the acquisition of artistic skills were the only ways in which the slave woman could gain visibility and be noticed by the harem master. "Odalisques with extraordinary beauty and talent," writes Alev Lytle Croutier, "were trained to become concubines, learning to dance, recite poetry, play musical instruments, and master the erotic art."[7] In this sense, the Turkish odalisque is very similar to the Japanese geisha, I told Hans, the latter being, to quote an expert, "used to describe girls or women who had acquired the skills of dancing and singing."[8] I then concluded my short speech by quoting Jahiz, a ninth-century Arab writer who in several essays analyzed the *jarya*'s predicament, declaring it completely irrational not to expect a talented woman to try to use her power and skills to dominate her master. The kind of love (*'isq*) inspired by a talented *jarya* "is a plague which reduces men to utter vulnerability," Jahiz explains, because she entraps men in a complicated emotional cocoon woven together out of multiple emotions operating at different levels. "This *'isq* includes and nurtures many kinds of affects," Jahiz notes. "It links together the feeling of love (*hub*), erotic passion (*hawa*), affinity (*mushakala*), and the inclination to keep the companionship going *(ilf)*."[9]

At this crucial moment of my recitation, just when I was expecting to reap some valuable information about Western men's psyches, the long queue in which we'd been standing vanished, and we found ourselves rushed into the opera house to deal with a more pressing issue: how to get to our seats when everyone else was already seated. And finally, once seated, all I could get from Hans was a sarcastic dismissal of Jahiz, who is one of my favorite authors.

"Fatema, how old was your Jahiz when he wrote this?" Hans said, taking me totally by surprise. "His concept of love is that of an adolescent. He expects too much: love, erotic passion, affinity, etc. . . . Have you heard of the Romantics? . . . Now we have to shut up." And that was that. Hans had just knocked down my beloved Jahiz, and I had to shut up because, unlike at the Rabat Mohamed V Theater, where you can continue conversing long after the curtain rises, here in Berlin we would have been thrown out if we had not focused on the show in rapt silence.

Well, actually, I am happy I did shut up, because it was after that memorable ballet, and the thought-provoking discussions it aroused, that I had my first inkling of the absence of fear of women in the Western harem. To my surprise, the ballet's Scheherazade lacked the most powerful erotic weapon a woman has—her *nutq,* or capacity to think in words and penetrate a man's brain by using carefully selected terms. The Oriental Scheherazade does not dance like the one I saw in the German ballet. Instead, she thinks and strings words into stories, so as to dissuade her husband from killing her. Unlike the Scheherazade in the German book I'd seen earlier, who emphasizes her body, the Oriental Scheherazade is purely cerebral, and that is the essence of her sexual attraction. In the original tales, Scheherazade's body is hardly mentioned, but her learning is repeatedly stressed. The only dance she performs is to play with words late into the night, in a manner known as *samar*.

*Samar* is one of the many Arabic words loaded with sensuality. Though literally, it simply means to talk in the night, it also implies that to talk softly in the darkness can open up incredibly rich veins of feeling. *Samar* reaches its perfect state when there is a moon; "the shadow of the moon" (*zil al qamar*) is, in fact, another meaning of *samar*. In the shadow of the moon, the lovers fade into their cosmic origin and become part of the shimmering sky. In the shadow of the moon, dialogue between a man and a woman—as difficult as it seems during the day—becomes a possibility. Trust between the sexes has a better chance to flourish when the conflicts of the day have faded. The Oriental Scheherazade is nothing without the fluid yet so intense hope of *samar*. You hardly pay attention to her body, so powerful is the spell of her fragile call for dialogue in the quiet night.

What on earth, I wondered as I remembered this, is the exact meaning of orgasm in a culture where attractive women are denied brain power? What words do Westerners use for orgasm if the woman's brain is missing? Intercourse is by definition a communication between two individuals; actually, in Arabic, one word for intercourse is *kiasa,* which literally means "to negotiate." And what has to be negotiated in sexual intercourse is the harmonization of expectations and needs, which can be accomplished only when the two partners use their brains. Scheherazade survived because she realized that her husband associated sexual intercourse with pain instead of pleasure. To get him to change his associations, she had to work on his mind. If she had danced in front of that man, he would have killed her as he had all the others before her.

When I consulted the Random House dictionary, I found that the English meaning of "orgasm" does not differ much from the Arabic. First, says the dictionary, orgasm means the physical and emotional sensation experienced at the culmination of a sexual act. Second, the word indicates an instance of experiencing this sensation. And third, orgasm refers to "an intense or unrestrained excitement." Both orgasm and excitement share the same Greek origin, whose meaning is to swell and literally expand beyond one's normal limits: *"orgasm(us),"* says the dictionary, "comes from the Greek *orgasmos,* excitement. *Orga(ein),* to swell, to be excited." At least one Arabic word for sexual pleasure has exactly that meaning: *"Ightilam,"* writes Ibn Manzur in his fourteenth-century Arab dictionary, "is to go beyond the limits, exactly like the ocean when it swells and its waves pound with a disturbed beat *(kal bahr haj wa dtarabat amwajuhu)."*

Communication is vital for achieving pleasure, for two individuals to take the risk to venture simultaneously beyond their own limits, at that very critical moment when regular beats are disturbed. So why does Scheherazade, the super-communicator, lose her ethereal dimension, her vaporous quality, when she travels West?

Is there a link between the fleshy nude painted by the German artist, the dancing Scheherazade of the German ballet, and the puzzling fearlessness of Western men in the harems of their Western minds?

Do Western men reduce seduction to body language?

Is seduction divorced from intense communication?

Who is the Scheherazade created by Western artists?

What weapons do men endow her with to enable her to seduce them?

But before figuring out who the Western Scheherazade is, we must first know a few things about the original Scheherazade. Only then will we be able to compare fantasies and learn from both cultures.

---

1. Alexander Dupouy, *Scènes Orientales* (Tubingen: Konkursbuchverlag, 1998).

2. N. M. Penzer, *The Harem: An account of the institution as it existed in the palace of the Turkish Sultans with a history of the Grand Seraglio from its foundation to modern times* (London: Spring Books, 1965), p. 13. First edition published by Harrap in 1936.

3. Ibn Hazm (Al Andalousi), "Man mata maqtulan mina l'khulafa" ("Those Who Died From Violent Deaths Among the Khalifes") in *Ar-Rassail* (*Short Essays*) (Beirut: Al Mouassassa al 'Arabia li-Dirassaat wa-Nachr, 1981), vol. II, p. 102.

4. The complete title of the book is: *Die Herrin Subeide Im Bade, order Von Der Geschlechter Lust und List in den Arabischen Nachten,* produced by Horst Lothar Teweleit, illustrated by Irmhild and Hilmar Proft (Cologne: Bund-Verlag, 1985).

5. Alev Lytle Croutier, *Harem: The World Behind the Veil* (New York: Abbeville Press, 1989), p. 9.

6. The Arab dictionary I will be using throughout this text is *Lissan al Arab,* literally "The Tongue of the Arabs," by Ibn Manzhur (Cairo: Dar al Maarif, 1979). The author Ibn Manzhur was born in Cairo in 1232 and died 1311.

7. Croutier, op. cit., p. 30.

8. Fernando Enriques, "The World of the Geisha," in *Prostitution and Society* (London: MacGibbon and Kee, 1962), Vol. II, p. 309.

9. Jahiz, "Kitab al Qiyan" ("The Book of the Singing Jarya") in *Ar-Rassail* (*Short Essays*) (Cairo: Maktabat al Khanji), vol. 8, pp. 166–167.

# 4

# The Mind as Erotic Weapon

Scheherazade is the Persian name of the young bride who tells the stories in *The Thousand and One Nights*. These stories are of "various ethnic origins, Indian, Persian, and Arabic."[1] The tales, which are a symbol of Islam's genius as a pluralist religion and culture, unfold in a territory that stretches from Mali and Morocco on the Atlantic Coast of North Africa to India, Mongolia, and China. When you enter the tales, you are navigating in a Muslim universe that ignores the usual borders separating distant and divergent cultures. For instance, in the tales, Persians speak Arabic and emerge as leaders in nations that do not share their cultural heritage. Scheherazade is the Arabic pronunciation of the Persian *tchihr*, which means "born," and *â zâd*, which means "to a good race"—in other words, aristocratic. Her husband, Shahrayar, is also Persian; his name is a contraction of the Persian words *shahr* and *dar*, meaning "owner of the kingdom."[2] Yet in her bedroom, Scheherazade does not speak Persian to her husband, a proud descendant of the Sassanian dynasty,[3] but rather narrates the tales in Arabic. And although Shahrayar is Persian, he "lived and ruled over the islands of India and Indochina."[4] However, the tales' cosmopolitan grace, their capacity to transcend cultural boundaries, does not extend to the relationship between the sexes. That is portrayed as an abysmal, unbridgeable frontier, a bloody war between men and women.

*The Thousand and One Nights* begins as a tragedy of betrayal and revenge, and ends as a fairy tale, thanks entirely to Scheherazade's intellectual capacity to read her husband's mind. When the stories begin, Shahrayar's younger brother, Shahzaman, is ruling happily over "The Land of Samarcand," only to return to the palace one day to find his wife in the arms of a "kitchen boy."[5] He kills the two of them and decides to leave his kingdom for a while, in the hopes of healing his wounds. He sets out to visit his older brother, Shahrayar.

Running away from the crime scene works for only a few days. One morning, the depressed Shahzaman looks out the window into his brother's harem garden and thinks he is hallucinating:

> While he agonized over his misfortune, gazing at the heavens and turning a distracted eye on the garden, the private gate of his brother's palace opened, and

there emerged, like a dark-eyed deer, the lady, his brother's wife, with twenty slave girls, ten white and ten black. . . . They sat down, took off their clothes, and suddenly there were ten slave girls and ten black slaves dressed in the same clothes as the girls. Then the ten black slaves mounted the ten girls, while the lady called, "Mas'ud, Mas'ud," and a black slave jumped from the tree to the ground, rushed to her, and, raising her legs, went between her thighs and made love to her. Mas'ud was on top of the first lady, while the ten slaves were on top of the ten girls, and they carried on till noon. Then the ten slaves put on the same clothes again, mingled with the girls, and once more there appeared to be twenty slave girls. Mas'ud himself jumped over the garden wall and disappeared, while the slave girls and the lady sauntered to the private gate, went in and, locking the gate behind them, went their way.[6]

The wife's sexual betrayal of her husband, King Shahrayar, reflects and mirrors the political betrayal of the master by the slave. In Arabic the sentence "Mas'ud was on top of the first lady" (*wa mas'ud fawqa a-sit*)[7] seems to sum up the entire harem tragedy: the woman's fatal need to topple the hierarchy built by the husband who has locked her up, by siding and copulating with his male slave. The woman's betrayal of her husband is built into the very structure of the

<u>harem</u>; it is the hierarchies and frontiers that men erect to dominate women that predetermine women's behavior. In the adulterous, criminal scene of *The Thousand and One Nights,* the harem frontiers are also porous, fragile. They can be easily blurred and erased; men can easily dress up as women and enter unnoticed.

But to get back to Scheherazade, she arrived at Shahrayar's palace years after the garden incident, by which time Shahrayar had killed not only his wife and her slave Mas'ud, but had also systematically beheaded hundreds of innocent virgins, marrying each one at night and killing them at dawn. "He continued to do this, until all the girls perished, their mothers mourned, and there arose a clamor among the fathers and mothers. . . ."[8] We see here once again how sex and politics mingle in the *Nights.* What started as a war between the sexes has turned into a tragic political upheaval, with bereaved fathers rebelling against the King. Now only one privileged father, the King's Vizier, who has carried out the death sentences, still had two virgin daughters: Scheherazade and her younger sister, Douniazad.

While the Vizier frantically tries to plot an escape for his daughters, Scheherazade insists on sacrificing herself and confronting the King in the hopes of stopping the killing. This is why Scheherazade can be seen as a political hero, a liberator in the Muslim world. "Father," she says to the distraught Vizier. "I would like you to marry me to King

Shahrayar, so that I may either succeed in saving the people or perish and die like the rest."[9] She has a scheme in mind that will prove to be successful: to weave spellbinding stories that will captivate the King, leaving him hungry to hear more—and save her life.

To change the mind of a criminal who is intent on killing you by telling him stories is an extraordinary achievement. In order to succeed, Scheherazade has to master three strategic skills: control over a vast store of information, the ability to clearly grasp the criminal's mind, and the determination to act in cold blood. The first skill is of an intellectual nature, requiring a wealth of knowledge, and Scheherazade's encyclopedic erudition is described in the first pages of the book: "Scheherazade had read the books of literature, philosophy, and medicine. She knew poetry by heart, had studied historical reports, and was acquainted with the sayings of men and the maxims of sages and kings. She was intelligent, knowledgeable, wise, and refined. She had read and learned."[10] But knowledge alone does not enable a woman to influence men in power; witness the enormous number of highly educated women involved in social movements in the West today, who are nonetheless unable to keep modern Shahrayars in check. Hence the interest in analyzing Scheherazade's highly successful story.

Our heroine's second talent is of a psychological nature: the ability to change a criminal's mind by using words alone. To use dialogue to disarm a killer is a bold strategy, and in order to succeed, the victim must have a good understanding of the criminal's probable moves and know how to integrate them into unfolding events, as in a game of chess. We have to remember that the King, the aggressor, does not talk to Scheherazade in the beginning. During the first six months of her storytelling, he keeps silent and listens without uttering a word. So Scheherazade has no way of knowing what is going on in his mind, except by watching his facial expressions and body language. How to continue talking in the night without making a fatal psychological miscalculation? Much like a military strategist, who uses his knowledge to foresee future events, Scheherazade has to guess, and guess accurately, because the slightest mistake will be fatal.

Scheherazade's final talent is her cold-blooded capacity to control her fear enough to think clearly and lead the dynamic interaction with the aggressor instead of being led. Scheherazade only survives because she is a super-strategist of the intellect. She would have been killed if she had disrobed like a Hollywood vamp or Matisse's odalisque and stretched out passively in the King's bed. This man is not looking for sex, he is looking for a psychotherapist. He is suffering from acute self-loathing, as we all do when we discover that we have been cuckolded. He is furious because he does not understand the other sex or why his wife betrayed him.

Despite her powerlessness, Scheherazade manages

through an accurate reading of a complex situation to change the balance of power and reach the top. This is why, even today, many women like myself who feel totally helpless in politics admire Scheherazade. Some Westerners who misread her story and reduce her to frivolous entertainer might view her as a bad role model for modern women. But I think that if you situate her accurately in her political context, her pertinence as a role model becomes quite clear. She saves not only herself but also an entire kingdom by slowly changing the mind of the chief decision-maker, the King. The British author A. S. Byatt is correct when she stresses that although the story "appears to be a story against women" at first, because of the enormous inequality between Scheherazade and her husband, the woman ends up completely taking over."[11] Ultimately, the King both renounces his macabre project of beheading his brides at dawn, and—through Scheherazade's subtle influence on his beliefs, motivations, and inner psyche— acknowledges that he was completely wrong in being angry with women. "O Scheherazade, you made me doubt my kingly power (*zahadtani fi mulki*) and made me regret my past violence towards women and my killing of young girls."[12]

This last sentence, in which a violent despot acknowledges that dialogue with his wife changed his entire world view, has inspired many famous twentieth-century Arab writers to grant Scheherazade, and by extension all women, the status of civilizing agents. Peace and serenity will replace violence in men's intentions and deeds, predicted the influential Egyptian thinker Taha Hussein, if they are redeemed by a woman's love. In his *Scheherazade's Dreams* (*Ahlam Scheherazad*), published in 1943, the storyteller becomes a symbol for the many innocents who were engulfed by the Second World War—a war that, while instigated by the West, also affected all Arabs and, indeed, the entire planet.[13] The King in Hussein's book symbolizes men's incomprehensible and tragic craving for killing. Only after listening to his captive for years does Shahrayar realize that she is a repository of a precious secret. If only he can grasp who she is and what she wants, he might achieve emotional growth and serenity:

> Shahrayar: Who are you and what do you want?
> Scheherazade: Who am I? I am the Scheherazade who offered you the pleasure of listening to my tales for years because I was so terrified of you. Now, I have reached a stage where I can give you love because I have freed myself from the fear you inspired in me. What do I want? I want my lord, the King, to have a taste of serenity. To experience the bliss of living in a world free of anxiety.[14]

Redemption, in Taha Hussein's work, starts when a dialogue is established between the powerful and the powerless. Civilization will flourish when men learn to have an intimate dialogue with those closest to them, the women who share their beds. Taha Hussein, who was blind, handicapped, and unfit to take part in wars—just like women—reawakened in the 1940s the symbolism inherent in the medieval Scheherazade tales—that linking humanism with feminism. Any reflection on modernity as a chance to eliminate despotic violence in the Muslim world today necessarily takes the form of a plea for feminism. Regardless of where you are, in Indonesia, Afghanistan, Turkey, or Algeria, when you zap through Muslim television or leaf through the written press, the debate on democracy soon drifts into a debate on women's rights and vice versa. The mysterious bond existing between pluralism and feminism in today's troubled Islamic world was eerily and vividly foreshadowed by the Scheherazade-Shahrayar tales.

In *The Thousand and One Nights,* Shahrayar officially admits that a man should use words instead of violence to settle his disputes. Scheherazade commands words, not armies, to transform her situation, and this adds yet another dimension to the tales as a modern civilizing myth. They are a symbol of the triumph of reason over violence.

Which brings me to emphasize a final point completely missing in Western artists' fantasies of Scheherazade. In the Orient, to use the body alone, that is, sex without a brain, never helps a woman change her situation. The

King's first wife failed miserably because her rebellion was limited to body politics—i.e., allowing the slave to mount her. Cuckolding her husband only traps a woman in a suicidal mission. But Scheherazade teaches that a woman can effectively rebel by developing her brain, acquiring knowledge, and helping men to shed their narcissistic need for simplified homogeneity. She teaches that there is a need to confront the different other, and to insist on the acknowledgment and respect of boundaries if dialogue is to be achieved. To learn to enjoy the fluidity of dialogue is to savor situations where the outcome of battle is not rigidly fixed, where winners and losers are not predetermined.

Abdesslam Cheddadi, a Moroccan historian and one of the most astute analysts of Islam today, states that the first key message of *The Thousand and One Nights* is that "Shahrayar discovers and becomes convinced that to force a woman to obey marital law is an impossibility."[15] But, adds Cheddadi, as revolutionary as this conviction is, it is less subversive than the tales' second message: If we admit that Shahrayar and Scheherazade represent the cosmic conflict between Day (the masculine as objective order, the realm of the law) and Night (the feminine as subjective order, the realm of desire), then the fact that the King does not kill the queen leaves Muslim men in unbearable uncertainty regarding the outcome of battle. "By allowing Scheherazade to stay alive, the King suspends the law he established himself," writes Cheddadi.[16] Paradoxically, it is Shahrayar, the male, who becomes paralyzed, by granting Scheherazade the right to live, speak, and thrive. "Law and desire balance each other and seem to come to a kind of suspenseful immobility, but with no guarantee that at any moment one or the other will resume its own movement."[17] At the end of the tales, men in the Muslim world can be sure of only one thing: The battle between the sexes, if representative of the battle between emotion and reason, has no end.

For Cheddadi, the Storyteller/King opposition in *The Thousand and One Nights* also reflects and magnifies the explosive conflict in Muslim culture between *Shari'a,* the sacred Truth, and Fiction. The triumph of Scheherazade is the triumph of *wahm* ("imagination") over the legitimacy of the keepers of *çidq* ("truth"); she corrodes their credibility.[18] Cheddadi then delineates the sad destiny of the *quççaç* ("street storytellers"), of which Salman Rushdie is a modern heir, and explains that their expulsions from mosques came about because the distinction between their fiction and "Truth" is a tricky one.

Street storytellers in medieval Baghdad were often branded as instigators of rebellion and, much like leftist journalists today, censored and banned from talking in public. In the Muslim year 279 (tenth century A.D.), states Tabari in his *History of Nations and Kings,* "The Sultan gave the order to inform the population in the City of Peace [a name for Baghdad] that no storyteller will be allowed to sit in the street or in the Big Mosque. . . ."[19] And Cheddadi explains the authorities' systematic witch-hunt of the storytellers by stating that the palace had no alternative but to silence these most dangerous of all creators: "Starting with the second part of the first century of Islam [7th century], we see Ali [the 4th Orthodox Caliph] expel storytellers from Basra Mosque. In the Orient, persecution of *quççaç* [street storytellers] will come to an end with their total extinction . . . , when they are replaced by the preachers (*mudhakkirun* or *wu'az*). It is the only way to establish a clear boundary between what ought to be considered as true and authentic and what pertains to the world of fiction, forgery, and lies."[20]

It goes without saying that the conflict between Truth and Fiction in the Muslim world is justified by another conflict, which brings us back to the conflict between Shahrayar and Scheherazade: If Truth is the realm of the law and its constraints, Fiction is the world of entertainment and pleasure. And to make the whole matter totally indigestible for fanatics, be they traditional or modern, Scheherazade, as Cheddadi reminds us, has an unsettling characteristic: "Scheherazade is introduced to us, from her first appearance in the book, with the credentials of a perfectly accomplished Faquih, a Muslim religious authority."[21] Her knowledge includes much history and an impressive mastery of the sacred literature, including the Koran, *Shari'a,* and the texts of various schools of religious interpretation.

It is this strange combination of enormous knowledge—learned from reading over one thousand books—and a seemingly unpretentious goal to stick to the world of the night and fiction, that makes Scheherazade especially suspect, and explains another strange phenomenon: For centuries, the Arab elite scorned her tales and did not bother to put them in writing.

To understand the emergence of the storyteller as a symbol of human rights in the modern Orient, one has to remember that for centuries, the conservative elite, with a few exceptions, scorned *The Thousand and One Nights* as popular trash of no cultural value whatsoever, because the tales were transmitted orally.[22] The male elite considered oral storytelling to be a symbol of the uneducated masses. Was that because the tales were mostly narrated by women within the private realm of the family? Although there is no conclusive scientific evidence to support this analysis, it is certainly a strong possibility and worth keeping in mind when trying to assess the peculiar place of the "feminine" *Thousand and One Nights* in our very "masculine" Muslim heritage.

Algerian-born Bencheikh, a contemporary expert of the Scheherazade tales, wonders if the vilification of the tales before modern times by labeling them *"Khurafa"* (loosely meaning "delirium of a troubled brain") was not due to the fact that women were often described as more astute than men.[23] In the logic of the tales, the judge is wrong and the victim is right. "The King is not only judged by Scheherazade, the victim, but is sentenced by her to change his ways according to her wishes. It is the world turned upside down. It is a world where the judge . . . does not escape his victim."[24] It is a world where the values are those of the Night. Remember the constant refrain that closes each of the tales:

Morning overtook Scheherazade (*wa adraka shahrazad ac̦-c̦abah*)
and she lapsed into silence (*fasakatat 'ani l'kalami l'mubah*).

When compared to the engulfing darkness of the night, the King's court and his justice system seem as fragile a mirage as the day. No wonder that the Arab elite, often encouraged and financed by their despotic rulers, condemned *The Thousand and One Nights* to oral history for centuries and prevented it from gaining the credentials of a written heritage. Not until the nineteenth century, one hundred years after the Europeans, who had the written text as early as 1704, were the tales finally published in Arabic! And none of the first editors was Arab!

The first edition of the Arabic text was published in Calcutta in 1814 by a Muslim Indian, Sheik Ahmad Shirawani, who was an instructor of Arabic at Calcutta's Fort William College. The second edition of the Arabic text is the 1824 Breslau (Germany) edition and the editor was Maximilian

Habicht. A decade later, Arab publishers began making money with the written text of the *Nights,* starting with the Egyptian Bulaq edition printed in Cairo in 1834.[25]

It is interesting to note that the first Arab editor of *The Thousand and One Nights* felt the need to interfere with the Bulaq version by "improving the language, producing a work that was in his judgment superior in literary quality to the original."[26]

What is puzzling, says the Algerian expert Bencheikh, reflecting on the special place of *The Thousand and One Nights* in our Muslim heritage, is that the storyteller does not deny women's *kayd,* their desire to sabotage men. According to him, this could explain why the Arab elites refused to write down the tales. "The storyteller, whose duty it was to obtain the grace of the cuckolded sovereign, put all her talent into creating tales that confirmed his distrustful feeling towards women."[27] The whole long string of tales are nothing but vivid illustrations of how sexually uncontrollable harem women are; to expect them to obey when inequality is enforced by law is preposterous.

Men can read their tragic destiny in each one of the tales, says Bencheikh. "We know that this terror of being betrayed has deep roots and exists in older cultures that expressed it more or less in the same way. . . . But here, we are working on a text written in the Arabic language. . . ."[28] The use of the Arabic language heightens tensions because it is the language of the sacred text, the

Koran. To write the tales down grants them a scandalously dangerous "academic" credibility. Modernity has brought Scheherazade to the center stage of the twentieth-century Arab intellectual scene, because long ago, in ninth-century Baghdad, she clearly articulated key philosophical and political questions that our political leaders still cannot answer today:

Why should an unjust law be obeyed? Because men have written it?

If Truth is so evident, why are imagination and fiction not allowed to flourish?

The miracle in the Orient is that it is Scheherazade's excessive thoughtfulness, together with her interest in wider philosophical and political issues, that made her explosively attractive. And the only way that Shahrayar could make sure that she was all his was to make love to her. Skillful lovemaking was the only tool he had to make her forget about the world for a few hours.

To seduce an intelligent woman who is concerned about the world, a man has to become the master of erotic art. When in the company of Scheherazade, Shahrayar's lovemaking reaches its full potential, which brings us back to the beginning: What happens to our queen when she goes West?

What changes do Western artists inflict on Scheherazade in order to make her conform to their fantasies when she crosses their frontiers?

What are the weapons of seduction with which Western artists equip her?

Does she become less or more powerful in their fantasy? Does she retain her status as queen, or lose it?

One thing is certain: We know the exact date Scheherazade crossed the frontier to the West: It was in 1704, and her first destination was Paris.

---

1. Introduction to *The Arabian Nights,* translated from Arabic into English by Husain Haddawy, based on text edited by Muhsin Mahdi (New York: Norton and Co., 1990), p. xi.

2. Hiam Aboul-Hussein and Charles Pellat, *Cheherazade, Personnage littéraire* (Algiers: Société Nationale d'édition et de Diffusion, 1976), p. 18.

3. The Sassanians were a prestigious dynasty of Persian kings who established a powerful empire from 226 to 641, until the conquest of Persia by Islam. When Islam appeared, the Sassanians and Byzantines were the predominant powers in the Near and Middle East.

4. Literally, "bi jazair al Hind wa Çin a Çin," on page 56 of Muhsin Mahdi's Arabic original of *The Arabian Nights* quoted above. The English translation is that of Husain Haddawy, op. cit., p. 3.

5. Literally, "wajada zawjatahu naima wa ila janibiha rajulan min çybiyan al matbakh," on page 57 of the Arabic original and page 3 of Haddawy's translation, op. cit.

6. Haddawy, op. cit., p. 5.

7. Haddawy, op. cit., p. 59.

8. Haddawy, op. cit., p. 9.

9. Haddawy, op. cit., p. 11.

10. Haddawy, op. cit., p. 11.

11. A. S. Byatt, "Narrate or Die: Why Scheherazade Keeps on Talking," in *The New York Times Magazine,* April 18, 1999, pp. 105–107.

12. "The Story of the Birds," which I have translated here, does not exist in al-Mahdi's version of *The Thousand and One Nights,* but does exist in one of the

cheapest and more popular versions of Scheherazade's tales, found in Morocco's souks (Beirut: al maktaba ach-cha'biya), vol. II, page 43.

13. Aboul-Hussein and Pellat, *Cheherazade, Personnage littéraire,* op. cit., p. 36.

14. Aboul-Hussein and Pellat, op. cit., p. 114.

15. Abdesslam Cheddadi, "Le conte-cadre des Mille et Une Nuits comme récit de Commencement." Contribution au "IV Colloquio de Escritorres Hispano-Arabe," Alméria, Spain, April 26–29, 1988. Page 11 of the manuscript generously shared by the author before its publication.

16. Cheddadi, ibid, p. 12.

17. Ibid., p. 19.

18. Ibid., p. 2.

19. Tabari, *Tarikh al Umam wa-l-Muluk"* (Dar al Fikr, 1979), vol. 6, p. 340.

20. Cheddadi, op. cit., p. 4.

21. Cheddadi, op. cit., p. 4.

22. The two exceptions of medieval historians who at least mentioned the tales in a few paragraphs (if only to remind Arabs about their Persian origin) were Mas'udi and Ibn Nadim. The ninth-century Mas'udi explained in his *Golden Meadows (Muruj Dahab)* that the tales were originally known by their Persian title, *"Hazar Afsane,"* literally the thousand tales. The tenth-century Ibn Nadim states in his *Fihrist* that, "The first to have created the tales . . . were the Persians of the First Dynasty. . . . The Arabs translated these tales, and talented men who had a literary gift recreated new ones and polished the old ones." In *Fihrist,* Flugel edition, 1871, p. 304, and p. 422 of the Cairo edition of 1929.

23. Jamel Ed din Bencheikh, *Les 1001 Nuits ou la Parole Prisonnière* (Paris: Editions Gallimard, 1998), p. 26.

24. Bencheikh, ibid., p. 34.

25. Hussain Mahdawi's introduction to *The Arabian Nights,* op. cit., xiv.

26. Hussain Mahdawi's introduction to *The Arabian Nights,* op. cit., xiv.

27. Bencheikh, op. cit., p. 29.

28. Bencheikh, op. cit., p. 32.04.

# 5

# Scheherazade Goes West

Scheherazade's first trip to the West was made in the company of a French scholar, Antoine Galland. An art collector who traveled to the Orient as secretary to the French ambassador, Galland was the first translator of *The Thousand and One Nights*. In 1704, at age fifty-eight, he became an instant success when he allowed Scheherazade to tell her stories in French, and he remained obsessed with translating her tales until his death in 1715. His twelve volumes took thirteen years to publish (1704–1717), two of them posthumously.

In the meantime, Scheherazade was achieving what the Muslims who had fought the Crusaders failed to do: She ravished the Christians, from devout Catholics to Protestants and the Greek Orthodox, using only words: "Versions of Galland appeared in England, Germany, Italy, Holland, Denmark, Russia, and Belgium. . . ."[1] The fact that the

French translator took the liberty of cutting out suggestive scenes and wondrous descriptions of lovemaking and female anatomy likely to shock his audience probably helped. After all, "Sultans, Viziers, and women of Arabia or India had to express themselves as one would if living in Versailles and Marly."[2] The subjugation of Christian souls by Scheherazade's tales was so satanically pervasive that ensuing translations and "pseudo translations," as scholar Husain Haddawy calls them, reached a staggering number. "By 1800, there were more than eighty such collections," he writes. "It was such hack versions that inflamed the imagination of Europe, of general readers and poets alike, from Pope to Wordsworth."[3]

Strangely enough, the intellectual Scheherazade was lost in all these translations, apparently because the Westerners were interested in only two things: adventure and sex. And the latter was expressed only in a bizarrely restricted form confined to the language of the female body. *Samar,* the Arabic word for talking late into the night, was nowhere to be found in the Christian Europeans' tales. For an entire century, Westerners' interest in *The Thousand and One Nights* was limited to its male heroes such as Sindbad, Aladdin, and Ali Baba. Scheherazade had to wait until 1845, when Edgar Allan Poe published "The Thousand and Second Tale of Scheherazade," to be celebrated as the brainy master of storytelling. I was very happy when I first heard about Edgar Allan Poe's sensible treatment of Scheherazade, and started looking for a copy of his book in Berlin bookstores. Poor Scheherazade had to cross the Atlantic, I thought, to find a man who would endow her with a developed intellect and describe her as "a politic damsel." From 1704 to 1845, she had gotten helplessly stuck in Versailles and the French court's obsession with women's fashion. In this respect, her initial connection with translator Antoine Galland had proven to be fatal to her reputation.

Versailles ladies were Galland's targeted audience. He even sought advice from duchesses and marquises before publishing his texts, which was probably one of the reasons he felt obliged to expurgate the tales. "I loaned my ninth volume of *The Thousand and One Nights* to Mademoiselle de Versamont so that she could read it to Madame the Duchess de Brissac . . . ," Galland noted in his diary on the second of February, 1709.[4]

One of the greatest fans of the Orient at that time was none other than the Marquise de Pompadour, Louis XV's official mistress, and she was more interested in harem clothes and the harem's fashionable luxuries than in women's subversive trends. In 1745, soon after Louis XV established La Pompadour in Versailles as his official mistress, she hung in her bedroom three paintings of *"Sultanes,"* or harem queens, by her protégé, artist Carle Van Loo. All three were beautifully bejeweled, well coiffed, and draped in luxurious clothes, thus forever linking harem women with frivolity and extravagant superfluous trifles.[5]

And, in 1778, on the eve of the French Revolution, Marie Antoinette herself appeared dressed as a "Sultane," which did not help one bit to restore poor Scheherazade's image as a political crusader fighting against despotic rule.

Besides adventure and sensual luxury, sexually explicit talk was the third element of *The Thousand and One Nights* that entranced early Western readers accustomed to being squeezed between censorious priests and cold rationalist thinkers such as Descartes.[6] The translations opened up the gates to an Orient where sexuality was boldly explored by a female storyteller forced to entertain a dangerous and sulky husband. This storyteller knew, centuries before the advent of satellite-wired "phone sex," that the most efficient weapon with which to arouse a man is words. That is the main lesson taught in "The Story of the Porter and the Three Ladies," which Scheherazade narrated to the King on their twenty-eighth night. Yet though her storytelling represents one of the most pornographic choices she could have made, the key message is a political one. Even when Scheherazade chooses to speak in the register of pornography, she has a political message to convey.

The story begins by describing the victim, a poor hardworking man, who is literally picked up by a rich woman. "I heard, O happy King," starts Scheherazade, "that once there lived in the city of Baghdad a bachelor who worked as a porter. One day, he was standing in the market, leaning on his basket, when a woman approached him. She wore a Mosul [mousseline, or fine muslin fabric] cloak, a silk veil, a fine kerchief embroidered with gold, and a pair of leggings tied with fluttering laces. When she lifted her veil, she revealed a pair of beautiful dark eyes graced with long lashes and a tender expression. With a soft voice and a sweet tone, she said to him, 'Porter, take your basket and follow me.' Hardly believing his ears, the porter took his basket and hurried behind her, saying 'O lucky day.' "[7]

In the Arabic text, the porter uses the word *qubul* for luck, and literally says, "How sexy I am today" (*ya nahari l'qubul*). Well, his self-flattering appreciation of the situation hardly prepares him to cope with what happens next. The lady instructs him to carry heavy jars of wine, loads of meats, bags of vegetables, and all sorts of dried fruits considered to be aphrodisiacs—raisins, figs, almonds, and hazelnuts—into a luxurious house that she shares with her two sisters. But once the job is done and the porter is paid a Dinar for his services, he refuses to leave. "Give him another Dinar," says one of the sisters, who was getting impatient. And that is when the porter reveals his intentions: Three beautiful women need a man.

"By God, ladies," he says, "my pay is not little, for I deserve not even two Dirhams, but I have been wondering about your situation and the absence of anyone to entertain you. For a table needs four legs to stand on, you being three, likewise need a fourth, for the pleasure of men is not complete without women, and the pleasure of women is not complete without men."[8]

But what the porter does not realize is that he will have to prove himself before the sisters will allow him to change his status from servant to sexual partner. After coldly reminding him that "Without gain, love is not worth a grain," the three ladies explain:

"You know very well that this table has cost us a lot and that we have spent a great deal of money to get all these provisions. Do you have anything to pay in return for the entertainment? For we shall not let you stay unless we see your share, otherwise you will drink and enjoy yourself with us at our expense."[9]

Well, what can make a poor man sexy? This is the tough question that the porter has to face, and he works to convince his hostesses that his intellectual capacity and sensitivity make him a superior lover.

"Trust me," he pleads. "I am a sensible and wise man. I have studied the sciences and attained knowledge; I have read and learned . . . and I am well-behaved."[10] And it is only then, after the porter has acknowledged that the giving and taking of sexual pleasure is a brainy task, that the sisters allow him to join in the party.

They start drinking wine and talking brilliantly into the night. Then the sister who first picked him up undresses and jumps into a lovely pool in the middle of the courtyard.

Then she washed herself under her breasts, between her thighs, and inside her navel. Then she rushed out of the pool, sat naked in the porter's lap and, pointing to her slit, asked,

"My lord and my love, what is this?"

"Your womb," said he.

"Pooh, pooh, you have no shame," she replied, slapping him on the neck.

"Your vulva," said he, and the other sister pinched him, shouting, "Bah, this is an ugly word." . . . And they went on, this one boxing him, that one slapping him, another hitting him. . . ."

The torture stops only when the porter finally understands the rule of the game: A man can never correctly name what a woman has between her legs. Only when the porter confesses that he does not know what to call a woman's sexual organ, and asks the ladies to help him, do the beating and slapping stop.

The porter then has to go through the same test with the other two sisters, both of whom also come out of the pool totally naked, jump in his lap, and ask the same question. Each time, he is beaten until he realizes that what is expected of him is to confess his ignorance concerning female genitalia. The message that he keeps forgetting is that it is foolish for a man to pretend to name what only a woman can control—her sex. For men to control what they cannot even adequately name is therefore pure delusion. This political dimension of *The Thousand and One Nights,* stressing female self-determination, helps to explain why, in the 1980s and 1990s, Egyptian fundamentalists repeatedly burned symbolic copies of the populist Arabic editions of the book, available in any medina for a mere 60 Dhs (6 dollars) for two volumes. And although no one knows how well the censored version of *The Thousand and One Nights,* which the fundamentalists then had printed, sold on the Egyptian market, what is certain is that in the Arab world no one mistakes Scheherazade's descriptions of sex for trivial pornography.

Which brings us back to our initial question: Why did the enlightened West, obsessed with democracy and human rights, discard Scheherazade's brainy sensuality and political message in their versions of the tales? Because when, two hundred years after Galland's translation, Scheherazade made a spectacular comeback in a twentieth-century Europe agitated with all kinds of revolutions and progressive ideas, she was again held hostage—this time by two Russian artists, Diaghilev and Nijinsky. Both used her to celebrate the body as the sole source of sexual pleasure, and achieved, in modern Paris, what Shahrayar had failed to do in medieval Baghdad—they silenced the storyteller.

Sergey Diaghilev had left his native Russia and come to Paris with his troupe, Ballets Russes, in 1910. His ballet *Scheherazade,* with costumes by Leon Bakst, then unleashed a continent-wide rage for harem-inspired fashion, especially the unforgettable harem pants, first designed by the French couturier Poiret. Poor Scheherazade was now condemned to exist only from the navel down. She had pants, yes, but no brain. She could dance, but Nijinsky was in control.

Vaslav Nijinsky rose to stardom as the golden slave in Diaghilev's ballet, *Scheherazade,* appearing "in brown body paint, and grinning, and wound with pearls—not so much as a sex object but as sex itself, with all the accouterments of perversity that the fin-de-siècle imagination could supply: exotism, androgyny, enslavement, violence."[12] Nijinsky's androgyny forced his admirers to focus on what men and women had in common. Yet insisting on the differences between the sexes, and forcing men to think about them, had been Scheherazade's unflinching, centuries-old message.

In addition, "the Ballets Russes unsettled gender norms. . . . The ballet companies were often characterized by a gender inversion of sexual power in which the dominant woman is desiring and the feminized man is desired."[13] This reversal of male-female power was totally antithetical to a dialogue between the sexes, which is what Scheherazade and her tales are all about.

Nijinsky's ballet also influenced Hollywood to overemphasize the purely sexual dimension of Oriental dance, and thereby blur its cosmic dimension, which can be traced back to the ancient Goddess cults. Many scholars believe that Oriental dance, also known as belly-dancing, was first developed by the Semites in the lustful temples of Ishtar, the goddess of love. "The Babylonian Ishtar in her oldest form is . . . a mother-goddess, unmarried, or rather choosing her temporary partners at will, the queen head and first-born of all gods."[14] To honor Ishtar and celebrate women's sovereign right to self-determination, devotees performed both dance and sex in her temples. With the fall of the Goddess cults, however, and the rise of the Gods, the women in the Ishtar temples were identified as sacred prostitutes. Therefore, millennia after the Goddess's defeat, it is not at all surprising that the sight of a woman dancing alone, as is usually the case in Oriental dance, stirs strange feelings and triggers incomprehensible anxieties.

In the Middle East and North Africa today, the belly-dance is seldom viewed, at least by women, as the mono-chromatic, physical agitation of the flesh, divorced from spirituality, that it is often portrayed as being in Hollywood films. In countries such as Morocco, the cults of goddesses like Venus and the Phoenician Tanit (both incarnations of Ishtar) thrived for centuries before the advent of Islam, and even today, semi-magic trance-dances are still being performed in caves all along the Atlantic Coast. During the religious festival of Moulay Abdalla, for example, celebrated a few kilometers from Casablanca, women play a key role in the ceremonies, defying the religious orthodoxy and its censors.

For centuries, mothers and aunts have taught little girls the elementary gestures of the Oriental dance as an exercise in empowerment. The dance is transmitted from generation to generation as a celebration of the body and a ritual of self-enhancement. For me, a writer who spends hours sitting in a chair, the Oriental dance is the only hobby and physical exercise I indulge in. I hate jogging and calisthenics and, like many of my female colleagues at the university, rush to the crowded Agdal fitness center at the end of the day to dutifully imitate the movements of Professor Magid, my favorite Egyptian dance instructor. The only thing that bothers me is that he pays more attention to the students than he does to us older professors. But you can bet that I always make some remark to ensure that all Muslims attending his class be treated equally. In an Arab world suffering from aggressive globalization, everything seems to be changing at vertiginous speed, except for women's stubborn need, regardless of age and social class, for a self-empowering dose of the trance-like Oriental dance. And this brings me back to our enigma: Why is this self-enhancing spiritual dimension of the Oriental dance missing in Hollywood's harems and representations of Scheherazade?

Hollywood's Orient, as portrayed in films such as *Kismet* (1920), *The Sheik* (1921), and *The Thief of Baghdad* (1924), was greatly influenced by the Russian ballets and costumes. The Ballet Russes, which toured the U.S. after its Parisian success, reduced the belly-dance to a series of trivial frills, with moments of a satanic perversity.[15] The feminine beauty that the movies projected was an often rather frightening "orientalized vamp"—a word that comes from "vampire."[16] Hollywood's favorite metaphor for the vamp's sexuality was that of a spider who entraps and destroys the hapless male. And of course the vamp does not encourage a man to engage in dialogue, but rather magnifies his fear.

Although many of the Western men I spoke with said that they had read an illustrated version of *The Thousand and One Nights* in childhood, it was the Hollywood films that seemed to have influenced them the most. Many men mentioned Universal's 1942 production of *Arabian Nights,* and invoked Maria Montez. This fiery actress specialized in Technicolor productions portraying the harem ladies as dressed in nothing but flimsy, transparent bras and skirts. But even when Maria Montez's star started to fade, the *Arabian Nights* genre, which primarily had to do with cabaret atmosphere, thrived for decades. Universal's *Arabian Nights,* writes historian Matthew Bernstein, "grossed several million dollars during World War II. It inaugurated a string of low-budget, Technicolor fantasies starring Maria Montez, with scantily clad harem women and brutally nasty despots (*Ali Baba and the Forty Thieves* and *Cobra Woman,* both in 1944, etc.). The formula was reproduced at other studios through the 1960s and upgraded in ancient and biblical wide-screen epics of the era, such as *Solomon and Sheba* (1959) and *Cleopatra.*"[17]

In addition to trivializing the belly-dance, the harem women traveling West also became associated with cosmetics. Body-beautification is a highly developed art in *The Thousand and One Nights,* where both men and women indulge in lengthy baths and perfume themselves in order to be more attractive. And this cosmetic dimension of Scheherazade's tales has had a more lasting and deeper impact on Western culture than their philosophical teachings. Harem-inspired cosmetics such as kohl and henna soon became part of the West's beauty secrets, reversing in at least one area the direction of colonization and transforming the conquerors into the conquered. "One indication of the prestige of the harem could be seen in the popularity of its beauty recipes," write Yvonne Knibiehler and Régine Goutalier, two women who have analyzed Western women's reaction to the Orient. "César Birotteau, Balzac's hairdresser, made a fortune selling his famous 'Mix of the Sultanes.' As for henna, kohl, and *ghassoul* (scented clay), they are still widely used in Europe today."[18]

In the early twentieth century, a whole series of harem beauty and cosmetic treatises flourished. One of the oddest is *Moroccan Harem Practices: Magic, Medicine and Beauty* by Mme A. R. de Lenz, the daughter of a French medical doctor who lived in Morocco in the 1920s. Lenz interviewed women about their beauty secrets,[19] but either because the interviewer had not mastered Arabic or because the women were not accustomed to being interviewed, most of their "secrets" appear to be just hilarious inventions—making the book highly entertaining. The West's fascination with harem beauty secrets lasted "until Pasteur and hygienic compulsion transformed the whole field into a scientifically-managed pharmaceutical business."[20]

In conclusion, one could say that the West's understanding of Scheherazade and the harem world was skin-deep, cosmetic and superficial. The storyteller's yearning for a dialogue between men and women found no echo in the West. And why, I kept wondering again and again, was this the case?

I was sitting quite exhausted in the Berlin airport, waiting for my flight to Paris, the last stop on my book promotion tour, and feeling sorry for myself for having made so little progress on my harem conundrum, when I had the bright idea to call Kemal. The day before, I had faxed him my first notes regarding the harem discoveries I'd made in the Berlin bookstores and at the *Scheherazade* ballet, and wanted to hear his reactions. I started looking for an available phone. I know that I am extremely homesick when I start squandering money on telephone calls to Morocco, and yet, I hesitated before making this call. It might be awkward to just ask Kemal out of the blue what he thinks of what I think of Western men's fantasies, I thought. Yes, maybe I should refrain from calling Morocco altogether.

Suddenly I felt thirsty—for guess what? I had a strong desire for a sip of strong mint-perfumed green tea served in a crystal glass. Yes, tea must be served in a crystal glass, as in Morocco, where much of the pleasure of drinking tea is looking at its golden color between sips. I was so involved in my mint-tea fantasy that I barely heard a message announced over the loudspeaker. My flight was running late, and I had at least an hour to kill. "I can't believe this," I mumbled to myself in Arabic. "It is as if Fate has created an unavoidable opportunity for me to call Morocco." But I should resist this kind of obscure intervention, I then thought, and not call. I should get a glass of tea instead. Yes. I stood up and very determinedly headed toward the nearest café-bar, where I ordered tea. A few minutes later, a cup of strong, black Lipton in a huge opaque cup was handed to me. That killed my desire for tea on the spot. Shuddering, I paid quickly and hurried toward the telephone booth.

"*Allo!* Kemal? *Labes?*" (*Labes* is the Arabic equivalent of "how are you." It literally means "no problems on sight?") "I miss you and I am homesick," I added quickly when I realized that there was only silence on the other end.

"It does not look as if you miss anyone in the Arab world, Fatema," came Kemal's delayed response. It is a bad sign when an Arab man sounds too calm and composed. "I gather from your notes that you are totally entranced by Western men. You are under their spell. You have written almost a whole book about them, so deep is your passion."

To have a fight while calling long distance is an expensive luxury. So I kept silent. Knowing Kemal as well as I do, I knew that he would soon feel guilty for being so impolite to me—poor creature that I was, so far away from sunny Morocco, in the harsh European climate. The silence worked.

"*Allo!* Fatema? Are you still there?" Kemal sounded very concerned now. "I am sorry to have been so rude. It must be cold over there." Then, after a minute of silence, he added softly, as if talking to himself, "Western men might not be as interesting as you think. They might be playing slightly different games, but they are just as scared of losing ground to women as we Arabs are."

"Kemal, what are you driving at? How is their game different?" I asked as calmly as I could. I was literally hugging the damn telephone. I knew Kemal too well. He had some interesting insights into my harem problem and knew that I was dying to know what they were. He knows me too well, too.

"Kemal, I am going to miss my flight," I said finally.

"Fatema." Kemal was speaking at last. "I think that you did not read Edgar Allan Poe's story through to the end, did you? As usual, you just buy books and expect others to read them for you."

"No, I did not," I confessed, a little embarrassed to admit that, so far, I had only skimmed the first paragraphs of the short story.

"The American writer assassinated Scheherazade," he

said. "What Muslim man would ever contemplate such a crime?"

I hung up and just stood there, suddenly feeling very lonely in that foreign airport.

Why on earth would Poe assassinate Scheherazade? I wondered. How strange Westerners are!

Cautiously, I boarded the plane, avoiding men's stares. But these men are Germans, I then reminded myself, not Americans. Yet who knows, I thought, maybe Edgar Allan Poe was of German descent—and they are all Anglo-Saxons, aren't they? Killing Scheherazade—what a horrible idea.

Will I feel safer in Latin Europe? I wondered.

---

1. Hiam Aboul-Hussein and Charles Pellat, *Cheherazade, Personnage littéraire* (Algiers: Société Nationale d'édition et de Diffusion, 1976), p. 20.

2. Introduction to *Le Livre Des Mille Et Une Nuit* (Paris: Robert Laffont, 1980), p. vi. Translated by Dr. J. C. Mardrus.

3. Husain Haddawy's introduction to his translation of *The Arabian Nights* (New York: Norton and Co., 1990), p. xiv.

4. "Le 2 Février 1709. Je prêtai mon IX° volume des Mille et Une Nuits à Melle de Versamont afin qu'elle en fit la lecture avec Mme la duchesse de Brissac . . ." Jean Gaulmer's introduction to *Les Mille Et Une Nuit,* translated by Antoine Galland (Paris: Edition Garnier-Flammarion, 1965), vol. III, p. 12.

5. Lynn Thornton, *La Femme dans la Peinture Orientaliste,* ACR Editions, Paris, 1985. Translated from the English by Jerôme Coignard, p. 6, p. 256.

6. Antoine Galland confessed in his journal that he much preferred the philosophy of Gassendi to Descartes. *"Il avait, nous dit son journal, 'plus de goùt pour la philosophie de Mr Gassendi que pour celle de Mr Descartes,' "* in Galland, *Les Mille Et Une Nuit,* op. cit., vol. III, p. 5.

7. Husain Haddawy's translation of *The Arabian Nights,* op. cit., p. 66.

8. Haddawy, op. cit., p. 70.

9. Haddawy, op. cit., p. 71.

10. Haddawy, op. cit., p. 71.

11. Haddawy, op. cit., p. 71.

12. Joan Acocella, "Secrets of Nijinski," in *The New York Review of Books,* Jan. 14, 1999, p. 54.

13. Gaylyn Studlar, "Out-Salomeing Salome," in *Visions of the East: Orientalism in Film* (Rutgers, N.J.: Rutgers University Press, 1997), p. 116.

14. Robertson Smith, *The Religion of the Semites* (New York: Schocken Books, 1972), p. 57.

15. "Most decisively of all for the cinema, Serge Diaghilev's Ballets Russes with its staging of Cleopatra, Thamar, and Scheherazade, which toured in the United States in the teens, contributed decisively to the mise-en-scène of Orientalist cinema," writes Matthew Bernstein in *Visions of the East,* op. cit., p. 4. The strong influence of the Ballets Russes on Hollywood is well described by Gaylyn Studlar in "Out-Salomeing Salome" in the same book.

16. Studlar, op. cit., p. 116.

17. Matthew Bernstein, op. cit., p. 11.

18. Yvonne Knibiehler and Régine Goutalier, *La Femme au temps des Colonies* (Paris: Stock, 1985). The exact French quote is on page 25.

19. Mme A. R. de Lenz, *Pratique des Harems Marocains: sorcellerie, médecine, beauté* (Paris: Librairie Orientaliste Paul Geuthner, 1925).

20. Knibiehler and Goutalier, op. cit., p. 25.

# 6

# Intelligence Versus Beauty

**P**oe killed Scheherazade in a horrible way in his "The Thousand and Second Tale of Scheherazade," and even claimed that she perversely enjoyed her own death: "She derived, however, great consolation during the tightening of the bowstring. . . ."[1] In Poe's story, Scheherazade had informed herself about many of the West's latest scientific discoveries, including sophisticated telescopes, the electro-telegraph, and the daguerreotype. But the King found these discoveries to be so unbelievable that he condemned her as a liar.[2] "Stop," he said to her. "I cannot stand that, and I won't. You have already given me a dreadful headache with your lies. . . . Do you take me for a fool? Upon the whole you might as well get up and be throttled."[3] To ignorant men, advanced scientific discoveries sound fictitious, hence Poe's famous subtitle "Truth is Stranger than Fiction."[4] But Poe's original idea, to turn

Scheherazade into an avant-garde broadcaster informing Muslims about the West's scientific inventions, would have enhanced her husband's military power and allowed him to end the West's occupation of the Orient. Scientific discoveries, after all, helped the West to equip its armies and occupy Muslim territories throughout the nineteenth century. When Napoleon successfully completed his swift second invasion of Egypt in 1801, his victory had more to do with the small crew of scientists who accompanied him than it did with his regular troops.

In Poe's story, Scheherazade calls upon Sindbad, now semiretired, to describe the latest technological achievements he had witnessed on his travels—inventions such as train engines and powerful telescopes revealing the secrets of the stars. If Shahrayar had listened, the Muslim world would have advanced faster and our Scheherazade would have survived. But instead, Poe betrays Scheherazade by making us associate her with Machiavelli and, even worse, with Eve. The corrupted Eve that is so central to Christianity does not exist in Islam, which has a much less misogynistic version of the Fall. For instance, the serpent who tempts Eve in the Bible does not exist at all in the Koran's version of the Fall.[5]

To make us suspicious of and ill-disposed toward Scheherazade, Poe cautions us that not only has the "political damsel" read Machiavelli, but also that she, "being lineally descended from Eve, fell heir, perhaps, to the whole seven baskets of talk which the latter lady, we all know, picked up from under the trees in the garden of Eden. . . ."[6] And, as if that was not enough, Poe then inflates Scheherazade's diabolical potential by making Eve look like a beginner. "In mentioning that Scheherazade had inherited the seven baskets of talk, I should have added that she put them out at compound interest until they amounted to seventy-seven."[7] With such a load to carry, no wonder the storyteller is doomed. But even more shocking to me is that Poe's Scheherazade accepts her death! She does not run away or try to dissuade her morbid husband with words. No! She accepts her death passively: "As she knew the King to be a man of scrupulous integrity, and quite un-likely to forfeit his word, she submitted to her fate with a good grace."[8]

Scheherazade's passive submission to her own death upset me so much that I could hardly carry on with the book promotion tour when I arrived in Paris. I was person-ally identifying with Scheherazade's horrible situation. A Muslim woman today is much like her: Words are the only arms she has to fight the violence targeted against her. Muslim men can afford to be fatalists, but Muslim women cannot. Before a Muslim woman consents to die, she must fight—Scheherazade said so. My grandmother Yasmina had told this to me many times and I believe it to be a sacred truth. Witness what happened in Iran following the Islamic Revolution: Iranian women were transformed into fearless street fighters. Writes Haleh Esfandiari, a former fellow at the Woodrow Wilson International Center for Scholars, who worked as a journalist in her native Iran, "They gained a new sense of themselves as women by refusing to be intimidated or cowed by the authorities, by being forced to wage a daily struggle over the right to work, by learning to develop subtle strategies for resisting the dress code, by having to fight in courts for rights of divorce."[9]

During my book tour, I realized how fragile I am and how many fears I have. Yet learning how to transform my fears into an initiative to dialogue is a drive I share with the medieval storyteller. Yes, I live and breathe in the new millennium and I own many modern gadgets, including a computer and a car, but my fears of violence are similar to those of the medieval Scheherazade. Like her, I have to face the daily threat of political violence unarmed. Only words can save me. This is why I was so scared by Scheherazade's American fate, and why, once in Paris, I could hardly admire the Seine River dancing along, so calm and so dignified. "That is what fear does," I thought. "It blinds you to the world's beauties."

I therefore decided to put myself through what I call "Arab psychotherapy." This simply means that you keep talking nonstop about your obsessions, even if people don't listen or care. One day, someone will give you a sensible observation or answer, and save you the trouble and expense of checking yourself into a psychiatric hospital. The only problem with this technique is that you lose a lot of friends. I almost lost the friendship of Christiane, my French editor, that way. An editor whose judgment I highly respect, she kept repeating that I was sabotaging my book tour by constantly talking about Edgar Allan Poe. "If you don't focus on yourself when you are being interviewed by journalists, don't expect them to do it for you," she said. "They are likely to write about Poe and forget about your book." Several times I promised Christiane that I would control myself, but of course I could not and kept raving about Poe and Western harems until I met Jacques, who treated me like a child by putting all his cards on the table.

"Let's focus on my interview first," he suggested, "so that I can write something for my magazine to earn my living. Then I will help you examine Poe's story and the harem enigma."

Although I found this proposition very logical, I could not help but react viscerally to his suggestion.

"You talk like an Imam or a caliph," I told him. "You will help me only if I accept your conditions. Can't you re-phrase your sentence more democratically—and be more explicit about the conditions you have in mind?"

"I can be more explicit about the conditions, yes," said Jacques. "I will do my best to help you by introducing you to my own private harem. I will give you a book to read first and then I will take you to two museums to meet my favorite odalisques. But in exchange for my precious contribution, you will have to introduce me to Harun Ar-Rachid and his harem. How does a caliph like him behave with his harem? I think that a pragmatic comparison between my harem and that of Harun Ar-Rachid will enlighten us both."

I agreed, thinking that it would not be a difficult task to introduce Jacques to Harun Ar-Rachid. Like many Arabs I know, I am helplessly attracted to this "sexy despot," as Kemal calls him, and have devoured all the medieval records describing his adventures in and outside the harem. I know everything about him, from what he liked to eat in ninth-century Baghdad to how he dressed, and, of course, all the details about his love affairs. All I needed to refresh my memory was a few hours in Paris's Bibliotheque National, where you can find the most precious of Arab manuscripts, stolen by French generals during colonization. I was absorbed in contemplating this ironic link between colonization and the circulation of knowledge when Jacques brought me back to reality.

"Now, to rephrase my suggestion more democratically," he said, while caressing his elegant Kenzo tie, "this is something I must request, even though you might object. The fun of a collaboration such as this, for a French citizen like myself, impoverished by the heavy taxes of the Republic, is to talk like Harun Ar-Rachid."

"What does that mean?" I asked, suspicious.

"It means that you don't interrupt me when I say something wrong," Jacques said solemnly. "You write down your corrections on a yellow Post-it and give it to me discreetly a few minutes later."

I could not help but explode with laughter at that, while thinking about how familiar his request was: Moroccan men also often display their vulnerability to get what they want. Is this something that all Mediterranean men share? I wondered, as I searched Jacques for Mediterranean traces. But I found none. He was an elegant man in his fifties, tall and thin but with a sensual paunch sticking proudly out, neatly trimmed sideburns, and cynical eyes so blue that they seemed like a genii's. However, those eyes were definitely not due to any genii connection, Jacques explained when I asked, but to his native Brittany. And that cynical touch that I had discerned was probably the result of "two divorces behind and many deceptions ahead." He then confessed that Christiane, my editor, would have been his ideal odalisque were she not so vain and conceited. When I asked him to be more explicit, he explained that she captivated the attentions of dozens of men, who were totally mesmerized by her. "Most of her male authors are more or less in love with her," he continued. "And so are we journalists, who rush to comment on the books she publishes, just to have the chance to drink a glass of champagne with her. So that gives you an idea of the extent of her harem."

Men are attracted to successful professional women in Paris, no doubt. But Jacques then explained that he could not stand the competition, and would ideally like to live with Christiane on a deserted island in the Pacific. Pulling out Ovid's *Art of Love,* a book that he said only men in Paris peruse nowadays, he read aloud a wonderful poem:

Lucky the man who can venture a bold defense of his
    loved one,
Lucky the man whom she tells, "I didn't do it!" (if
    true.)
Made of iron, or mad, or a masochist, no doubt
    about it,
Such is the fellow who craves proof beyond shadow
    of doubt.
But I saw you, I say, and I was perfectly sober,
Though I know what you thought—I was both drunk
    and asleep.
I was watching both, I saw you waving your
    eyebrows;
I could tell what you said when you were nodding
    your head.
And your eyes were not dumb, nor the scribbles you
    made on the table,
Dipping your fingers in wine, each of the letters a
    sign.
Oh, and the double talk, too, under the innocent
    meanings,

Messages broadcast in code—don't think I
   misunderstood.[10]

I was baffled by Ovid's poem, largely because it sounded
so Arabic to me. Jacques was just like Kemal—so insecure
and vulnerable, and yet irresistible. Ovid's poem strongly
reminded me of a popular 1980s poem put into music by
Egyptian singer Abdelwahab, whose words men all over
the Arab world could be heard humming whenever their
partners were late. "Don't lie! I saw you both together. . . ."
(*"La takdibi, ini ra'aytukuma ma'an"*). I sang the song for
Jacques, who reacted by telling me that things have not im-
proved much since Ovid was born, in 43 B.C. And then we
returned to the harem enigma.

Art history was Jacques's field, and I was eager for him to
take me to the Paris museums and show me his favorite
painted harems. His interest in the Orient gave him, as he
put it, "the distance needed to reflect intelligently on the
Parisian fate and also to fly to Marrakech when it snows on
the home front." He was also the youngest of three children, the others both girls, which he joked would be
Freud's explanation for the reason behind his harem addiction.

Like many sensitive men, Jacques's humor was his
armor. It gave him that unsettling charm that also makes
Arab intellectuals irresistible: You can never be sure
whether they are serious or joking. They keep you guess-

ing, and whenever you do go ahead and decide that they are serious, you soon discover that you are wrong. This kind of man discourages a woman from investing too heavily in him. It is not unusual for an Arab man to make you open up like a rose by repeating three times in a row that you are wonderful, and then forget all about you thirty minutes later. To jump to the conclusion that he is madly in love with you is suicidal.

When I discussed Jacques's charm with Christiane, she cautioned me against him. "As a journalist he has impact," she said. "If he writes about a book, thousands of French citizens will rush to buy it. But as a man, I would not trust him." When I asked her to elaborate, without of course telling her about Jacques's secret plot to whisk her away to an uninhabited island, she said that editors work closely with journalists: "We form a modern harem right here in the middle of Paris, my dear." I pressured her to be more explicit, and she replied that Jacques was a ridiculously jealous man who had trouble coping with modern women—he was *"Un macho sympathique."* I then managed to make Christiane laugh when I retorted that in Rabat, I feel comfortable with macho men who express their negative feelings toward women openly. "It is the others who trigger my suspicion and drive me to the verge of paranoia," I said.

After this conversation with Christiane, I decided to go along with Jacques's conditions. I let him grill me for his article and was relieved when it appeared in print on schedule. Then, Jacques started my initiation into his harem. His first step was to force me to read a mysterious book that he handed me in a café on the Rue de Rivoli, facing the Louvre. "This is the ideal café for self-torturing intellectuals," he said as we met. "It has luxurious red-leather banquettes, huge ceilings that swallow the noise, and strong espresso. I will pick you up in two hours to meet my first odalisque. Two hours is enough for you to read this book. "

The book he handed me was Immanuel Kant's *Observations on the Feeling of the Beautiful and Sublime.* The only way to understand Westerners, Jacques said before he left, is to read their philosophers. He then asked me if I knew Immanuel Kant. Since I never lie to hide my ignorance, because to do so is to miss fantastic opportunities for learning, I confessed bravely that I never read him. All I knew was that he was German and an important thinker whom all cultivated Europeans quote frequently. Jacques was amazed at my ignorance and asked me what I was required to read in high school. I replied that my primary education had been devoted to learning the Koran by heart, and my secondary years, to reciting pre-Islamic poetry. My chances of meeting Immanuel Kant in my native Fez had therefore been nil. At that, Jacques laughed and added that maybe that was a good thing, because Kant was not particularly nice to women. He was, however, key to understanding

Edgar Allan Poe's assassination of my storyteller, and a good way to begin exploring the Western harem enigma.

According to Kant, a "normal" woman's brain is programmed to "the finer feeling." She must relinquish "the deep understanding, abstract speculations, or branches of knowledge useful but dry" and leave them to men. Writes Kant: "Laborious learning, even if a woman should greatly succeed in it, destroys the merits that are proper to her sex, and because of their rarity they can make of her an object of cold admiration; but at the same time they will weaken the charms with which she exercises her great power over the other sex."[11] This discovery of Kant's split between beauty and brains scared me at first. What a terrible choice Kant's woman has to face, I thought—beauty or intelligence. It is as cruel a choice as the fundamentalists' threat: veiled and safe, or unveiled and assaulted. I wished I could throw away the unsettling book and just enjoy myself in the Paris café without obsessing about why men and women everywhere have so much trouble being happy together. But then I remembered Yasmina's remark that travel is not about fun but about learning, about crossing boundaries and mastering the fear of strangers, about making the effort to understand other cultures and thereby empowering yourself. Travel helps you to figure out who you are and how your own culture controls you.

Reading Immanuel Kant opened up new horizons for

me. As I sat in that Rue de Rivoli café on that memorable morning, new questions rushed to my mind about both the West and the East, questions I later shared with both Jacques and Christiane, my Parisian mentors.

Kant's message is quite basic: Femininity is the beautiful, masculinity is the sublime. The sublime is, of course, the capacity to think, to rise higher than the animal and the physical world. And you'd better keep the distinction straight, because a woman who dares to be intelligent is punished on the spot: She is ugly. The tone in Kant's book is as cutting as that of a Muslim Imam. The only difference between an Imam and Kant, who is considered to be "the chief luminary of the German Enlightenment,"[12] is that the philosopher's frontier does not concern the division of space into private (women) and public (men) realms, but into beauty (women) and intelligence (men). Unlike Harun Ar-Rachid, a caliph who equated beauty with erudition, and paid astronomic sums for the witty *jarya* in his harem, Kant's ideal woman was speechless. For not only does great knowledge wipe out a woman's charm, according to Kant, but exhibiting such knowledge kills femininity altogether: "A woman who has a head full of Greek, like Mme Dacier, or carries on fundamental controversies about mechanics, like the Marquise de Chatelet, might as well even have a beard."[13] Madame Dacier (1654–1720) translated the *Iliad*, the *Odyssey*, and other Greek and Latin classics into French, and the Marquise de Chatelet, the companion of Voltaire, won a prize in 1738 from the French Academy of Science for an essay on the nature of fire.[14]

I felt that I had stumbled on a radical difference between the East and West. As far back as I can remember, I have always been told, either directly when I committed a blunder or indirectly through a tale, that a stupid woman gets nowhere. I thought of Tawaddud, a science wizard and one of Scheherazade's heroines. Yasmina, who was illiterate, would often ask one of my older, educated cousins to read that tale to me to make sure that I got the message right:

The Caliph asked Tawaddud:

"What is your name?" to which she answered,

"My name is Tawaddud." He then inquired,

"O Tawaddud, in what branches of knowledge dost thou excel?" to which she answered,

"O my lord, I am versed in syntax and poetry and jurisprudence and exegesis and philosophy; and I am skilled in music and the knowledge of the Divine ordinance and in arithmetic and geodesy and geometry and the fables of the ancients . . . and I have studied the exact sciences, geometry and philosophy and medicine and logic and rhetoric and composition; and I have learnt many things by rote and am passionately fond of poetry. I can play the lute and know its gamut and notes and notations and the crescendo and diminuendo. If I sing and dance, I seduce, and if I dress and scent myself, I slay. In summary, I have reached a pitch of perfection such as can be estimated only by those of them who are firmly rooted in knowledge."[15]

In this dialogue between the master and the slave, Tawaddud tries to sell herself. The few minutes of attention that the Caliph grants her is her chance to compete not only with the other women in the harem but also with all the male scholars and artists swirling around the palace, hoping to entertain the ruler. A harem woman had no other alternative but to invest in her intellect. To follow Kant's advice, and cultivate intellectual mediocrity, would have been suicidal.

According to Kant, women should not study geometry, astronomy, or history—all disciplines considered vital for any ambitious harem beauty who wanted to keep up with her caliph. Writes the philosopher: "Their charm loses none of its strength even if they know nothing of what Algarotti has taken the trouble to sketch out for their benefit about the gravitational attraction of matter according to Newton."[16] Algarotti was a count who in 1736 wrote a simplified summary of Newtonian optics, *Newtonianismo per le Dame*, addressed to women, on the premise that they were incapable of digesting the original.

In addition to mathematics, history and geography are two other disciplines that can demolish a woman's beauty, according to Kant: "In history they will not fill their heads with battles, nor in geography with fortresses, for it becomes them just as little to reek of gunpowder as it does the male to reek of musk."[17] And as for geography, a woman should know just enough to keep up with an entertaining discussion, but not enough to display any serious knowledge: "For the ladies, it is well to make it a pleasant diversion to see a map setting forth the entire globe or the principal parts of the world. . . . [But] it is of little consequence whether or not the women know the particular subdivision of these lands, their industry, power, and sovereigns. Similarly, they will need to know nothing more of the cosmos than is necessary to make the appearance of the heavens on a beautiful evening a stimulating sight to them, if they can conceive to some extent that yet more worlds, and in them yet more beautiful creatures, are to be found."[18]

Isn't it strange, I thought upon reading this, that in the medieval Orient, despots like Harun Ar-Rachid appreciated defiantly intelligent slave-girls, while in enlightened eighteenth-century Europe, philosophers like Kant dreamt of silent women! Such a bizarre separation between feeling and reasoning! In Kant's enlightened West, the world is not populated by a single race of humans who share the capacity to feel and think, but by two distinct kinds of creatures: those who feel (women) and those who think (men). A woman in his enlightened West is a creature whose "philosophy is not to reason, but to sense."[19]

What does all this mean? I wondered as I sat in the café.

Is this why Poe assassinated Scheherazade? Is this why Western men are so euphoric in their harems?

Yet at least Poe granted Scheherazade an unusual brain. Three years earlier, the French writer Théophile Gautier had also killed Scheherazade in his novella *La Mille et Deuxième Nuit* (1842). But he killed her because she had run out of inspiration.[20] Poe killed her because she knew too much.

Why do Western and Eastern men dream of such different beauty ideals and what does the beauty ideal tell us about a culture?

Why would a progressive Western man like Kant, who was so concerned about the advance of civilization, want a woman with a paralyzed brain?

Could it be that the violence against women in the Muslim world is due to the fact that they are acknowledged to have a brain, while in the West, they are often considered to be incapable of deep or analytic thought?

At this stage, I suddenly felt very sick. I had heart palpitations. I looked outside to see if Jacques was back, and then remembered that he was always late, just like Moroccans. I looked at my watch: fifteen minutes more until our appointment. I know why I am sick, I thought, it's half due to Kant and half due to the three coffees I just drank. I kept forgetting that everything in the West, starting with its coffee, is much stronger than at home. Well, I would have to see a doctor about my heart palpitations. It would be such a hassle to have a heart attack in France, because I would like to be buried in Temara Beach, near Rabat. I then remembered that I had no written will and had not purchased my tombstone, as is traditionally done in Fez. All I had was "Maroc-Assistance," an insurance that would ship me back home if I died in Christiandom. I shook myself—I had to stop these depressing thoughts, and had better take care of these matters as soon as I got back. But in the meantime, as Yasmina would say, "A woman should start with her easiest problems. Eliminate the small things you control." So I ordered a healthy orange pressée and had just started to enjoy it when Jacques appeared.

Our first destination was the Musée du Louvre, where Jacques's oldest odalisque dwells, and our second, to the Musée du Centre Pompidou, home to his youngest. "I am not as lucky as the caliphs who could shove all the women they loved into one harem," said Jacques. "In Paris, a man is forced to visit various museums regularly in order to piece together his harem."

Before entering the Louvre, Jacques changed his colorful Kenzo tie for a huge dark bow tie. "A man has to be extremely elegant and irresistibly handsome when stepping into his harem," he said, and then dashed with a royal swagger through the museum's entrance.

---

1. From "The Thousand and Second Tale of Scheherazade," in *Tales of Mystery and Imagination,* by Edgar Allan Poe (London: Everyman's Library, 1998), pp. 332–349.

2. For details on the scientific discoveries described by Poe, see notes 6 and 7 on page 346 and note 3 on page 348, ibid.

3. Ibid., p. 349.

4. Ibid., p. 332.

5. D. Sidersky, *Les Origines des Légendes Musulamanes dans Le Coran* (Paris: Librairie Orientaliste Paul Geuthner, 1933), p. 14. For the Koran verses concerning the Fall, see Sura 7:18–22 and Sura 20:121.

6. Poe, op. cit., p. 334.

7. Poe, op. cit., p. 334.

8. Poe, op. cit., p. 349.

9. Haleh Esfandiari, *Reconstructed Lives: Women and Iran's Islamic Revolution* (Washington, D.C.: The Woodrow Wilson Center Press, 1997), p. 7.

10. Ovid, *The Art of Love,* translated by Rolfe Humphries (Bloomington, Ind.: Indiana University Press, 1957), p. 46.

11. Immanuel Kant, *Observations on the Feeling of the Beautiful and Sublime,* translated from the German by John T. Goldthwait (Berkeley, Calif.: University of California Press, 1991), p. 79.

12. Ibid., p. 2.

13. Ibid., p. 79.

14. Ibid., notes 1 and 2 on page 121.

15. "The Story of Abu al Husn and his slave girl Tawaddud," from *The Book of the 1001 Nights and a Night,* translated by Richard F. Burton (London: Burton Club for Private Subscribers, 1886), vol. V, pp. 193–194.

16. Kant, op. cit., p. 79.

17. Kant, op. cit., p. 79.

18. Kant, op. cit., p. 80.

19. Kant, op. cit., p. 79.

20. Not only did Gautier turn Scheherazade into a sterile storyteller who had lost her inspiration, but he also made her come to Paris to beg him to write new tales for her. But the King does not like the story that Gautier writes, and Scheherazade is killed, just like all the other brides before her. Gautier, *La Mille et Deuxième Nuit* (Paris: Le Seuil, 1993), p. 256.

# 7

# Jacques's Harem: Unveiled but Silent Beauties

Once inside the Louvre, Jacques became very solemn and said that we now had to follow his sacred harem ritual. "First, I visit my harem baths," he said, "so that I can see all of my beauties together. It makes it easy to count them and to make sure that no one has escaped. Then, I visit my favorite wife and we admire each other undisturbed." With that, I understood that I was not supposed to ask too many questions, so as not to interrupt his dream, and quietly followed him upstairs. Here, he stopped in awed silence in front of Jean-Auguste-Dominique Ingres's *Turkish Bath,* where more than twenty nude odalisques have been splashing in an intimate palace pool since 1862. The serene, relaxed atmosphere of the painting seemed familiar, reminding me of the *hammam,* or public baths, that I go to back home to forget about research and academic strife. Ingres, who never set foot in the

Orient, had nonetheless managed to capture the baths' most important quality: the simple, pure sensuality that comes with taking off your clothes and relaxing in a warm misty room.

*Hammams* once flourished in the Islamic world and especially in medieval Baghdad. In the eleventh century, the scholar Hilal al-Sabi tried to establish how many baths existed in the city and was baffled by the astronomical estimates offered by the people he interviewed. "We found many among both the upper classes and the commoners who believed that the baths numbered 200,000 or more," he wrote. "Some others said there were 130,000 baths, and others claimed 120,000. . . ." But eventually, after much sophisticated calculation, the author settled on 60,000 as the most likely number.[1]

Deriving tremendous pleasure from the mere cleaning of one's body, and turning it into sensual ritual, constitutes one of the major differences between Muslim and Christian cultures. Pampering oneself in a *hammam,* by massaging your tired skin for hours on end with fragrant *ghassoul* (clay perfumed with herbs), has absolutely nothing to do with the ascetic world of the Western sauna, which I experienced while in Stockholm, Sweden. There, I did not dare use *ghassoul* because the place was as clean as a surgical ward.

From the start, Christianity condemned bathing as a lustful sin. "What of those who frequent promiscuous baths, who prostitute to eyes that are curious to lust, bodies that are dedicated to chastity and modesty?" warned Cyprian, the Bishop of Carthage, as early as A.D. 200. "Such washing defiles, it does not purify nor cleanse the limbs, but stains them. . . ."[2] It is true that in Cyprian's time, men and women frequented the public baths together, a legacy from the Roman tradition, when the baths "became little more than well-conducted brothels."[3] But this connection between the public baths and promiscuity is totally absent in Muslim culture, where, from the beginning, the strict separation of the sexes was the rule. In medieval Baghdad, the emphasis in the single-sex baths was to clean the body with a narcissistic sensuality that excluded paying attention to anyone else.

Descriptions of bathing abound in *The Thousand and One Nights,* and baths are often used as preparatory rituals to important acts involving the crossing of new frontiers in time or space. When a traveler enters a new city, when a foreign woman enters a new palace, or when a youth is about to embark on a night of pleasure—all begin their journeys in the *hammam.* Since this conception of the bath as a cleansing ritual is completely lacking in Christian culture, it is not especially surprising that many Western artists were drawn to what they regarded as an exotic Oriental fantasy. In fact, it was not until the time of the Crusades that Westerners discovered the purely hygienic dimension of the bath. "Whatever inheritance the Dark

Ages in Europe possessed," writes Fernando Henriques in *Prostitution and Society,* "an emphasis on bodily hygiene was no part of it. It was not until the Crusades that Europe, adapting the idea of the Oriental *hammam,* began to appreciate the advantages of a public cleansing of the body."[4] For centuries, however, even this discovery did not change the Westerners' strangely phobic attitude toward the baths. Historian Norbert Elias tries to explain this attitude by pointing out that many Westerners associated the baths with the danger of contracting the infectious diseases that plagued medieval Europe. "The idea that water is dangerous was transmitted from generation to generation," he writes. "As a result, one finds suspicious if not repulsive reflexes toward baths and ablutions."[5] Thus, in the Western mind, to enjoy oneself in the bath had long been linked with terrifying dangers, be they sinful sex or devastating epidemics.

Ingres's imaginary *Turkish Bath* looked "normal" to me at first, because most of the women in the painting were not looking at one another, which is also usually the case in the Oriental *hammam.* We Muslim women don't rush to the baths to look at our neighbors, and I myself don't like to stare too much at who is sitting near me because I am likely to encounter a colleague from the university or one of my students or the wife of my building's janitor. The rule in the Rabat baths is to concentrate on scrubbing off your dead skin with a harsh cloth, replenishing your oils with *ghassoul,* and then applying a light layer of henna paste to give your skin a nice hue. You avoid talking to your neighbors because it will spoil your concentration on sensuality. This atmosphere of complete self-absorption is also strong in Ingres's *Turkish Bath.* Each of his odalisques is looking at some vague point on her narcissistic horizon, totally self-centered—probably the major reason, by the way, why women spend more time in *hammams* than do men; it is the only place where they are not asked to serve food or perform services for someone else. But what reminded me that Ingres's *Turkish Bath* depicted a territory foreign to me was the fact that two of the women were erotically caressing each other. That would be impossible in a Moroccan *hammam* for the simple reason that it is a public space, often overrun with dozens of noisy children. Erotic pleasure in Morocco belongs in preciously sheltered private places. Like many of my compatriots, I am always amazed when I see Western men and women kissing each other in the streets, because for us, erotic intimacy does not belong out in the open, but is a miracle that one must protect in cocoon-like privacy. Yet when I shared this idea with Jacques, who was still staring at the Ingres, he said that as far as he was concerned, as long as there were no other men in sight, women could do whatever they wanted in his *hammam.* "Fatema," he said, "you have to understand that when I step into my harem, even those women who are caressing each other will immediately stop what they are doing and turn to me. That is why this painting gives me so much joy."

The painted harem has another valuable quality that Jacques reminded me of as we rushed downstairs to the Salle Denon to meet his favorite odalisque. "Economics is where Western men are more clever than Muslim men," he said. "My harem is paid for by the French Republic. Imagine how much it would cost me if I had to entertain and keep all those naked women by myself. And the taxes I would have to pay! Here, it is the duty of the Republic to take care of the paintings in expensive museums so that I can keep my fantasy going. All I have to do is put on my bow tie whenever I decide to visit these lonely ladies waiting in the dark to hear my steps." I could not help but laugh at that, but I had to refrain from chuckling too loudly, because we had just arrived at Jacques's favorite harem lady, Ingres's *La Grande Odalisque,* finished in 1814.

Immediately, I realized that I already knew the woman very well—she has been endlessly reproduced on book covers and in art magazines as the epitome of erotic beauty. Jacques told me that the best description he has ever read of her "indescribable" charm was that of the American Robert Rosenblum, a professor of fine arts at New York University. "An idle creature of the harem," quoted Jacques, "whose feet have never been wrinkled or sullied by use, the odalisque is presumably displayed passively for our delectation. . . . She reclines in padded luxury, fondled by satins, silks, furs, and feathers."[6] After that, Jacques stopped talking and disappeared into a silent reverie, his hand caressing his bow tie. But he was not the only one admiring her; dozen of other men, many of them tourists, were standing nearby, whispering in all kinds of European languages, from Finnish to Croatian, as they admired *La Grande Odalisque*. The shimmer of her skin was magnified by the darkness inside the huge, high-ceilinged room, and except for her turban and a feather with which she was fanning herself, she was totally nude. The painter had caught her from the back, at a vulnerable moment when she had turned her head, as if hearing footsteps behind her. Nudging me, Jacques murmured that the combination of nudity and vulnerability was one of the secrets of the magic spell of *La Grande Odalisque*.

Jacques then added that meeting La Grande Odalisque had been one of the defining erotic moments of his sexual education. For his generation, he said, seeing nude women in real life had been close to impossible while growing up. Only when introduced to the history of art did boys and young men see nude women for the first time.

"I was eleven when Soeur Bénédictine, my teacher at our neighborhood Catholic school, took us to the Louvre one Saturday afternoon," he said. "And she must have noticed my confused sexual awakening because she murmured softly in my ear, 'Dear little one, don't look so intently at the paintings.' "

Yet I found the odalisque's nudity to be troublesome. In

Muslim harems, as I explained to Jacques, women are not nude. Only crazy people go about naked. Not only do women in harems keep their clothes on all the time—except to go to the *hammam*—but they often dress like men, in trousers and short tunics. And in fact, the first Europeans who were lucky enough to glimpse a sultan's court were very surprised by the androgynous silhouettes of the women. The Frenchman Jean Thévenot, for example, already startled to see that harem women were not veiled, was shocked to discover that they "dressed just like men," and described in detail the agile movements that the harem pants and short tunics allowed.[7]

The first Christian to describe a Turkish sultan's seraglio, or harem, was Thomas Dallam, sent from England to Constantinople in 1599 on a very special mission: to make sure that a precious organ, a gift to the sultan from the King of England, worked properly.[8] Dallam arrived in Constantinople in August, and for a month, the sultan allowed him daily access to the seraglio in order to install the musical instrument. Although he was not allowed to go beyond the men's courts, and was forbidden entrance to the harem, Dallam did manage to catch a glimpse of the sultan's concubines playing in their well-protected court one day. And to his amazement, he discovered they were dressed like men:

> When I came to the grait the wale was verrie thicke, and
> graited on bothe the sides with iron verrie strongly; but

through that graite I did se thirtie of the Grand Sinyor's concobines that weare playinge with a bale in another courte. At the firste sighte of them I thoughte they had bene yonge men, but when I saw the hare of their heades hange doone on their backes, platted together with a tasle of smale pearle hanginge in the lower end of it, and by other plaine tokens, I did know them to be women, and verrie prettie ones in deede.[9]

These reactions of early Westerners to glimpses of the harem led me to think that in the West, men rely more on fashion to establish their distance from women, and more consciously emphasize their power through clothing. In the Orient, in contrast, in countries like Morocco, men and women even now still wear traditional clothes in the evening (Western clothes are identified with work), with the difference between the male and female *djellabas* residing more in details and choices of color. When I explained this to Jacques, he agreed that we had stumbled on a major difference between our two cultures.

"In my harem, I prefer my women to be totally nude, just like Ingres's *Grande Odalisque,*" he said in a ceremonious tone that censored any type of dissension. "Nude and silent— these are the two key qualities of my harem women."

"This is really bizarre," I finally dared to comment, but only after we had left the Salle Denon and were heading toward the exit. "Muslim men seem to get a sort of virile power from veiling women and harassing them in the streets if they aren't 'covered' properly, while Western men like yourself seem to derive a tremendous pleasure from unveiling them."

Jacques said that he had never thought about it that way before, but agreed that both nudity and clothing provided important clues when tracking down the different ways in which men imagine beauty and pleasure in the East and West. "One thing is for sure," he added. "My odalisque cannot leave her room if I deprive her of her clothes. I don't have to lock the door. She will never dare to step outside if I make sure she is totally nude.

"And besides," he concluded when we were in his car heading toward le Centre Georges Pompidou to meet the last of his favorite odalisques, who lived in the Musée National d'Art Moderne, "depriving women of their clothes greatly reduces the cost of maintaining a harem in Paris."

As we neared the final member of Jacques's harem—Matisse's *Odalisque à la culotte rouge* (Odalisque with Red Trousers)—he once again became mystically silent. "Here is my second favorite odalisque, after the Ingres," he whispered as he stood in awed admiration in front of the painting. He then bowed elegantly to her, and turned his head just in time to catch the smiles of the crowd of tourists around us, who were sharing his pleasure. But I felt sorry for the poor odalisque: Except for her red culottes hanging loosely around her hips, she was wearing nothing but a completely open chiffon shirt, which left her breasts awkwardly bare. Lying vulnerably on a low mattress, with her arms behind her head and the drapes around her pushed to the background, she seemed totally exposed. She looked sad and lonely, lost in her own thoughts.

I said to Jacques that I would not describe her as being beautiful because she looked so troubled, and he agreed that there was something strange about her extreme vulnerability.

"Maybe insecure men like myself are attracted to that," he mumbled. "Our emotions are such a mystery." He then added that it had taken him a long time to choose this as his favorite odalisque from among the many that Matisse had painted. For a while, he had thought that the artist's *Odalisque à la culotte grise* who dwelt in another Parisian palace, the Musée de l'Orangerie, not so far away, was seductiveness incarnate. And before that, when he was younger, Jacques confessed with a sly smile, he had been smitten with the *Odalisque with Raised Arms* (1923), now at the National Gallery of Art in Washington, D.C.

"Matisse must have run out of culottes when he got to her," Jacques said, "because she has nothing on but transparent white chiffon, draped around her ample hips. Plus she wears an extraordinarily dreamy gaze that makes you want to wake her up." At one point, Jacques added, he had even considered switching harems altogether—to those of Picasso. Surprised, I confessed that I had never heard of Picasso painting odalisques and harems. But Jacques said that the modernist's odalisques were "oozing" with brutal sex. "Picasso painted no less than fourteen harems and drew numerous sketches between the end of 1954 and the beginning of 1955," he said. "They are known as variations of Delacroix's *Femmes d'Alger dans leur appartement*."[10]

Just as we were about to leave the room, I noticed that *Odalisque with Red Trousers* was finished in 1921, and I had what the Sufis call *lawami'*, or an enlightening flash. That date is important in Muslim history, as it is the year when women's liberation occurred in Turkey, as part of a nationalist struggle for liberation. In the 1920s, when Matisse was painting Turkish women as harem slaves, Kemal Ataturk was promulgating feminist laws that granted Turkish women the right to education, the right to vote, and the right to hold public office. As a consequence of those laws, which were to transform the entire Muslim world, no less than seventeen women were elected to the 1935 Turkish parliament—the first representative body ever to be democratically elected in Turkey, which up until then had been ruled by the powerful Ottoman dynasty.

Throughout the 1920s, Turkey had been the site of a radical struggle waged by a movement known as the "Young Turks," who fought against three things perceived to be intimately linked: despotism, sexism, and colonization. The Young Turks, led by Ataturk, blamed the sultan's despotic rule for Muslim "backwardness," which had led to widespread Western occupation. The Young Turks also attacked the harems and the seclusion of women, arguing that illiterate mothers could not help but produce ill-prepared sons and daughters. In 1909, the Young Turks banned the harem and the Turkish sultan was forced to free his ex-slaves—now citizens of the first republic in Muslim history. The Turkish civil code adopted in 1926 also outlawed polygamy, and gave equal rights of divorce and child custody to both men and women. Women's enfranchisement soon followed, with women granted the right to vote in local elections in 1930, and in national elections in 1934.[11]

"Kemal Ataturk campaigned against the veil and forced feminist reforms as a strategic component of nation-state building among the countries of the Middle East and Europe," writes Denitz Kandiyoti, a leading Turkish expert on women.[12] This connection between democratization and feminism as a way to end colonization then reverberated throughout the Muslim world, from Morocco to Pakistan, producing a widespread concern for women's education and other reforms. The first Moroccan schools for girls, which I attended, opened in the 1940s, and were the result of a similar nationalist movement. Ataturk's reforms and military successes also succeeded in halting the European advance on Turkish territories, making him a hero for many. Therefore, the passive Turkish women that Matisse painted in the 1920s are more French than they are Turkish, as they existed in his fantasies only.

Yet somehow, I thought dispiritedly as I studied the painting, the Frenchman's odalisque seems to be more powerful than reality, because even now, eighty years after Ataturk, many Westerners still believe that in the Orient, things never change. They believe that Muslim men and women never dream of reform or aspire to be modern.

I kept looking at the 1921 date inscribed on *Odalisque with Red Trousers,* dumbfounded that a Western painting, an image created by Matisse, could keep Turkish women in slavery, when in reality, they were entering politics and the professions. Could it really be that an image has more power than reality? I wondered. Is reality that fragile?

This idea of the image as a weapon that condenses time and devalues reality made me very uncomfortable. If the West has the power to control time by manipulating images, I thought, then who are we if we do not control our own images? Who am I—and who makes my image? I couldn't even begin to answer these questions, and since some strange truths need time to be digested, I tried to make myself relax, to spend a whole day gazing at the magnificent Seine. I owe it to myself, I thought, to forget about all these bizarre musings and just enjoy the sensuous feeling of being alive. Too many women have lost the drive to be happy because they become obsessed with analyzing their situation.

That memorable afternoon with Jacques, I clearly saw

the invisible link between three seemingly disparate things: Kant's ideal of the brainless beauty, the power of the painted image, and Western movies. All three are major weapons used to dominate women in the West, I realized, and the image is a way to condense time. It does not matter if in actuality Turkish and European women in the 1920s were liberating themselves; in much of Western imagination, Matisse and others like him were in control of both time and female beauty. In the Orient, men use space to dominate women; Imam Khomeini, for example, ordered women to veil when stepping into public space. But in the Occident, men dominate women by unveiling what beauty ought to be. And if you don't look like the picture they unveil, you are doomed. Is this what Kemal was insinuating when he suggested that Western men use something besides space to control women? Could it be that here men achieve power over women by manipulating time via images? What a strange contrast between the two cultures.

When I shared these strange ideas with Christiane a few days later, she gave me a tiny book, which she said was as important to understanding the Western concept of beauty as was Kant—*De Pictura* by Leon Battista Alberti, written in 1435. Alberti, Christiane said, was a Renaissance man who identified the painted image as one of the foundations of Western civilization and explored its power to subjugate time. "Painting possesses a truly divine power," Alberti wrote, "in that not only does it make the absent present (as they say of friendship), but it also represents the dead to the living many centuries later."[13] No wonder, Alberti went on, philosophers like Socrates and Plato, as well as emperors like Nero, Valentinianus, and Alexander Severus, "achieved distinction in painting."[14] But there was also another important link that Alberti made, Christiane said, which was pertinent to the enigma of the Western harem: the connection between the painted image and the creation of something of value. Writes Alberti: "How much painting contributes to the honest pleasures of the mind, and to the beauty of things, may be seen in various ways but especially in the fact that you will find nothing so precious which association with painting does not render far more valuable and highly prized. Ivory, gems, and other similar precious things are made more valuable by the hand of the painter. Gold too, when embellished by the art of painting, is equal in value to a far larger quantity of gold."[15]

A third thing that struck me when I read Alberti was that slaves in Greece were forbidden to paint. "The excellent custom was especially observed among the Greeks that free-born and liberally educated young people were also taught the art of painting together with letters, geometry, and music. . . . The art was held in such high esteem and honored that it was forbidden by law among the Greeks for slaves to learn to paint."[16]

So maybe there is no perverse connection between the

painted image and time as war-machine after all, I thought. But if there were one, the euphoric smiles that the word "harem" evokes among Westerners would be more comprehensible; since the male artist controls the image of beauty, his harem is a safe place, filled with nude and silent women. It does not matter much if, in actuality, the women do have brains and are intelligent, as long as they hide it. It is a question of role-playing and theater—just like with the veil. The fanatics who force women to veil in Afghanistan, Algeria, and elsewhere do not denigrate women's intelligence; instead, their war is about access to public space. Men have to keep the monopoly over the streets and the parliaments; women have to veil to show they don't belong. Veiling is a political statement.

When stepping into the street, the veiled woman agrees to be a shadow in the public space. Power manifests itself as theater, with the powerful dictating to the weak what role they must play. To veil on the Muslim side of the Mediterranean is to dress as the ruling Imam demands. To be considered beautiful on the European side of the Mediterranean is to dress as the market-Imam commands. It might be an interesting therapy, I thought, for both men and women in the East and West to switch cultures and roles in order to clarify what is going on. Maybe I should seriously consider creating a travel agency during my retirement, to help people dance between cultures. But before doing so, I had better make sure that my theory is right. Otherwise, I will go bankrupt the first year.

But how do I make sure that I am right? I asked myself. I guess I must just carry on bombarding foreigners with questions.

What happens to women who refuse to conform in the West?

Women who do not conform to Kant's image of the silent beauty will be punished as ugly—or worse. Edgar Allan Poe's assassination of Scheherazade now seems totally logical, even the norm. If intelligence is the monopoly of men, women who dare to play clever will be stripped of their femininity. How sophisticated and how subtle! Kemal is right: Western men are cleverer than Muslim men. In this kind of war zone, no blood needs to be spilled.

Thinking just such thoughts had given me a headache and abruptly ended my visit to Jacques's harem. I asked him to drop me off in front of my hotel. He was sorry to hear of my plight, but reminded me of my promise to introduce him into Harun Ar-Rachid's harem.

Yes, I will, I agreed—but only after I get some rest. Tomorrow, I will go searching for fragrant mint tea and couscous in the twentieth arrondissement, where there is a large concentration of Arab immigrants. I need to get a taste of my native medina. I am feeling homesick. I miss the sun and the drinking of mint tea in the late afternoons, with the muezzins of the minarets frantically chanting the end of the day. Maybe diving into Arab history and Harun Ar-Rachid's Baghdad will help me too.

---

1. Hilal al-Sabi, *Rusum dar al Khilafa* (Rules and Regulations of the Abbasid Court), translated by Elie Salem (Beirut: American University of Beirut, 1977), p. 21. Hilal al-Sabi died in 448 of the Muslim calendar, A.D. 1056.

2. Fernando Henriques, *Prostitution and Society* (London: MacGibbon & Kee, 1962), vol. II, p. 15.

3. Ibid.

4. Ibid., vol. II, p. 56.

5. Norbert Elias, *La Civilisation des Moeurs,* French translation of *Uber den Prozess der zivilization,* which appeared in 1939 (Calmann Levy, 1973), p. 280.

6. Robert Rosenblum, *Ingres* (New York: Harry N. Abrams, 1990), op. cit., p. 86.

7. Jean Thévenot, *Voyage du Levant* (Paris: F. Maspero, 1980), op. cit., p. 123.

8. N. M. Penzer, *The Harem* (London: Spring Books, 1965), p. 32.

9. Thomas Dallam, *Early Voyages and Travels in the Levant* (London: Hakluyt Society, 1893), p. 74. Dallam visited Constantinople in 1599.

10. "Delacroix, la Couleur du Rêve No. 1" (Paris: Bibliothèque Des Expositions, Issued on the occasion of the Delacroix Exhibition at the Grand Palais, April 10–July 20, 1998), p. 55. For more on Picasso's erotic series from a woman's point of view, see Rosalind Krauss, "The Impulse to See," in *Vision and Visuality,* edited by Hal Foster (Seattle: Bay Press, 1988), pp. 51–78.

11. Denitz Kandiyoti, "From Empire to Nation State: Transformations of the Woman Question in Turkey," in *Retrieving Women's History: Changing Perceptions of the Role of Women in Politics and Society* (Paris: UNESCO, 1988), p. 219.

12. Ibid.

13. Leon Battista Alberti, *On Painting* (New York: Penguin Books, 1991), p. 60.

14. Ibid., p. 62.

15. Ibid., pp. 60–61.

16. Ibid., p. 63.

# 8

# My Harem: Harun Ar-Rachid, the Sexy Caliph

When I think of the harem, my imagination drifts to the first two Arab dynasties, the Umayyad (661–750), whose capital was Damascus, and the Abbasid (750–1258), whose capital was Baghdad. Both dynasties ruled the Muslim empire after the death of the prophet Mohammed in the year 11 of the Muslim calendar (632 of the Christian calendar).[1] Despite there having been fifty-one Arab caliphs during the reign of these first two dynasties, only one comes rushing to my mind: Caliph Harun Ar-Rachid.[2]

The name Harun Ar-Rachid has been triggering the imagination of countless Arabs ever since his reign in the ninth century. He inspired many of the tales from *The Thousand and One Nights* because of his magical combination of qualities: physical beauty, youth, athleticism, intelligence, love of learning and the sciences, and military success. Harun Ar-Rachid also seems to have had a rich emotional and sexual life. He was not afraid to love, to express his emotions, or to explore the passionate feelings that women stirred in him. Harun Ar-Rachid often confessed that when a man falls in love and expresses his emotions, he becomes vulnerable and jeopardizes his capacity to control women. But this capacity to express his feelings and admit his vulnerability when in love is one of the secrets of Harun's lasting spell. I, myself, like everyone else, am of course scared of making a fool of myself by declaring my love to a man who might not care for me at all. Whence my admiration of Harem Ar-Rachid's courage to show his emotions and run the risk of being ridiculed. In at least one of the tales in *The Thousand and One Nights*, he is described as an unfortunate husband, betrayed by an unfaithful *jarya* who seduces his own musician.

Harun Ar-Rachid was born on February 16, 766 (the year 149 of the Muslim calendar), in Rayy, a Persian city whose remnants lie a few miles south of present-day Teheran. By all accounts he was handsome without being superficial or conceited. This is a rare combination, at least on my side of the Mediterranean. Medieval Muslim historians—who are, of course, all male—describe his good nature as being due to a harmonious mix of physical characteristics and intellectual gifts: "Ar-Rachid was very fair, tall, handsome, of captivating appearance and eloquent. He was versed in science and literature. . . ."[3] He also believed that the agility of the mind depends on the agility of the body, and that both must be developed through games and competitions. Harun Ar-Rachid "was the first Caliph to popularize the games of polo, shooting with the bow in the course of a tournament, ball games, and racket games. He rewarded those who distinguished themselves in these various exercises and these games spread among the people. He was also the first among the Abbasid Caliphs to play chess and backgammon. He favored the players who distinguished themselves and granted them pensions. Such was the splendor, wealth, and prosperity of his reign that they called this period the 'Days of the Marriage Feast.' "[4]

But if Harun Ar-Rachid had been nothing more than a handsome, chess-playing prince, he would have been forgotten or dismissed as a negligible entity, like many of today's oil-rich playboys. In contrast, Harun knew when to stop playing and switch to business. One of the key words of Arab civilization is *wasat,* which simply means the midpoint between two extremes; we are taught since childhood to aim for striking a balance between reason and passion. And Harun's life was in perfect balance. In addition to his highly developed intellectual and physical capabilities, "he was scrupulous in fulfilling his duties as a pilgrim and waging Holy War. He undertook public works by building wells, cisterns, and strongholds on the road to Mecca. . . . He strengthened the frontiers, built cities, fortified several towns . . . carried out innumerable works of military architecture, as well as building caravansaries and ribats. . . ."⁵

The ideal ruler is one who puts his people's solidarity at the top of his agenda and does not hesitate to use his own money if necessary to help those who are in trouble. Harun's chief enemies were the Christians, and "in the year 189 [810 of the Christian], he ransomed his people with the Romans, so that there did not remain a single Muslim captive in their territories."⁶ But even this would not have been enough to keep the caliph's memory alive for generations, if he had not also attacked the Roman Empire: "In the year 190 he took Haraclea and spread his troops over the Roman territories."⁷ Containing Christian aggressiveness made Harun the ideal Muslim leader, and his famous letter to the Roman emperor Nikephoros, who breached a contract, is taught to all Muslim children in kindergarten. "In the name of God, the Merciful and the Compassionate, from the servant of God, Harun, Commander of the Faithful, to Nikephoros, the dog of the Romans, as follows: I have understood your letter, and I have your answer. You will see it with your own eye, not hear it."⁸ Then he sent an army against the Romans.

Ar-Rachid sent his impassioned letter to the Emperor because the Roman had refused to honor a treaty made between his mother, Queen Irena, who ruled from 797 to 802, and Harun, when he invaded Byzantium. Nikephoros, categorically rejecting his mother's treaty, had written: "From Nikephoros, the King of Romans, to Ar-Rachid, the King of the Arabs, as follows: That woman put you and your father and your brother in the place of kings and put herself in the place of a commoner. I put you in a different place and am preparing to invade your lands and attack your cities, unless you repay me what that woman paid you. Farewell!" And when that letter reached the caliph, he was so furious that he decided to lead the Muslim army himself, and not desist until Nikephoros was defeated: "Ar-Rachid advanced relentlessly into the land of the Romans, killing, plundering, taking captives, destroying castles, and obliterating traces, until he came to the narrow roads before Constantinople, and when they reached there, they found that Nikephoros had already had trees cut down, thrown across the roads, and set on fire. . . . Nikephoros sent gifts to al-Rachid and submitted to him very humbly and paid him the poll tax for himself as well as for his companions."[9]

But again, if Harun Ar-Rachid had been nothing more than a fighter, he would not have survived in people's imagination for centuries. It was his capacity to know when to stop fighting, enjoy life, and cultivate sensuality and refined entertainment that made him a hero. He also became a hero because he was young (he was twenty-one when he became caliph, and died at the age of forty-four), had a strong erotic dimension, and was not afraid to explore it. This romantic side is captured in many of the stories of *The Thousand and One Nights*.

The first woman whom Harun fell in love with, at age

sixteen, was his cousin Zubeida, herself a proud princess. He married her right away in a ceremony that took place in a fabulous palace called Eternity (*Al-Khuld*). "People came from all horizons," writes Ibn Khalikhan, one of the more restrained historians of the period. "Huge sums of money, the likes of which Islam had never before seen, were distributed at this occasion."[10] Various chronicles give minute details of Ar-Rachid's love for Zubeida and of the luxuries that he showered her with while she was the favorite. "She was the first to be served on vessels of gold and silver enriched with precious stones," writes one ninth-century observer. "For her the finest clothes were made of the varicolored silk called *washi,* a single length of which, designed for her, cost 50,000 dinars. She was the first to organize a bodyguard of eunuchs and slave girls, who rode at her side, fulfilled her orders, and carried her letters and messages. She was the first to make use of palanquins of silver, ebony, and sandalwood, decorated with clasps of gold and silver. She was the first to introduce the fashion for slippers embroidered with precious stones and for candles made of ambergris—fashions which spread to the public."[11] But in spite of Zubeida's vanity and love of luxury, Muslim historians never dismissed her as a brainless creature. Instead, they always stressed her interest in the environment and in public works; it was Zubeida who was responsible for the building of waterworks on the roads linking Baghdad to Mecca, to ease the pilgrims' travel. That young

Harun had chosen as a wife a princess who was both beautiful and politically involved was to be expected.

In spite of his love for Zubeida, as soon as Harun Ar-Rachid became the fifth caliph of the Abbasid dynasty, he found himself surrounded by *jarya* from all over the world. Their talents and elegance excited historians: "Ar-Rachid had 2000 jarya . . . ," wrote one. "Some were experts in singing. . . . And they were covered with jewelry."[12] Since at that time Muslims were not supposed to enslave fellow Muslims (though they did later in history), most of the *jarya* were foreign women from newly conquered territories and the variety of their talents was magnified by the diversity of their origins. Foreign *jarya* who wanted to become singers had an arduous road ahead of them; besides learning voice and various instrumental techniques, they also had to master the Arabic language, with its difficult grammar, and compete with home grown stars like Fadl. Considered to be the epitome of beauty, Fadl set the standards for Arab singers for centuries to come. Writes one historian: "Fadl was dark-skinned, well versed in literature (*adiba*), eloquent, with an extraordinary sense for quick, witty answers (*sari'at al hajiss*), accurate in her poetry rendering."[13] Another describes Fadl's ability to speed up the rhythm of dialogue and surprise her partners by introducing unexpected linguistic nuances—something much appreciated in Arab culture to this day. "Fadl was among the most beautiful of Allah's creatures. She had excellent calligraphy, surpassed everyone in eloquence when it came to words, and was a perfectly skillful communicator (*ablaghuhum fi mukhataba*), clear when engaged in a discussion. . . ."[14]

To be a foreigner in the Abbasid court was not really a drawback, however, since the culture encouraged diversity and rewarded people for speaking many languages and bringing the richness of their own backgrounds into their performances. In fact, during the Abbasid dynasty, "scholars, artists, poets, and *littérateurs* came from a variety of ethnic backgrounds (speaking Aramaic, Arabic, Persian, and Turkish), colors (white, black, and mulatto), and creeds (Muslim, Christian, Jew, Sabian, and Magian). It was this cosmopolitanism and multiculturalism of Baghdad that made for its enduring strength as a great center of culture."[15] According to Jamal Eddine Bencheikh, a modern expert on seduction in medieval texts, the price of a first-rate singing *jarya* in the eleventh century was 3,000 dinars, while the yearly pension of a well-known poet such as Ibn Zaidun was 500 dinars, and a construction worker earned one Dirham a day. With one Dirham, one could buy three kilos of bread.[16]

The more skills a *jarya* commanded, the more varied the sensuous pleasures she could offer the master, and the more she was worth. This is one of the most striking features of the Abbasid harems during the dynasty's Golden Age. Slave dealers knew what kind of women were likely to please each caliph, as in the case of Mamun, Harun Ar-

Rachid's son, who inherited the throne after him: "I heard a slave-dealer say as follows: I showed a slave girl to al-Mamun, skilled in versifying, eloquent, well-bred, and a good chess-player, and I asked of him a thousand dinars as her price and he said, if she can cap a verse I will recite to her by a verse of her own, I will purchase her for what thou askest, and will give thee over and above the bargain."[17] Caliph Mamun especially enjoyed playing chess with a woman. He practiced the game to sharpen his mind and prepare for war, but playing with a woman also gave him an added sensuous thrill. He believed that only if the players engage in a game body and soul does intellectual competition reach an exciting edge, and he considered it more appropriate to say "Come, let us press one another" than "Come, let us play."[18] That competition has an erotic dimension for the competitors is considered common knowledge today, but it must have been quite a startling thing to say during Caliph Mamun's time.

One fourteenth-century writer, Ibn Qayyim al-Jawziya, who took the trouble to count up the words in Arabic that can be used to say "I love you," came up with a list of sixty, which he compiled into a book, *Garden of Lovers* (*Rawdat al Muhibbin*). An analytic mind of infinite refinement, al-Jawziya remarked that having so many words with which to express the same thing was not a particularly good sign, but rather implied that there "was a problem." The Arabs, he explained, usually make an effort to name only complex concepts so abundantly—i.e., only those difficult to grasp (*ma chtadda al fahmu lahu*) or treacherous to their hearts (*aw katura khuturatuhu 'ala kulubihim*). In any case, he added, having so many words for a single concept was, in fact, one way to celebrate an important civilizing phenomenon (*ta'diman lahu*). On his list were many words that refer to love as a dangerous moment of mental confusion (*khabal*), or disorientation (*futun*). There is also the concept of love as a plunge into the void (*hawa*), similar to the English "fall in love" or the French *tomber amoureux,* and words that equate love with madness (*junun, walah, kamad*) or atrocious suffering (*tadlih, wasb, hurqa, chajan*). But to me, the most interesting revelations of al-Jawziya's list, which cheer me up and sustain my hopes, are those that describe love in positive terms—as a privileged friendship where tenderness facilitates communication (*khilla, mahabba*) or provides a strong bolt of energy.

Though love as energy is central to the Sufis, it is also a concept open to ordinary people like you or me who have no spiritual pretensions. "A man in love will give prodigally to the limit of his capacity, in a way formerly he would have refused . . . all this in order that he may show off his good points, and make himself desirable," writes Ibn Hazm, an eleventh-century politician and expert on religious law who devoted a book to the mysteries of emotions. "How often has the miser opened his purse-strings, the scowler relaxed his frown, the coward leapt heroically into the fray, the clod suddenly become sharp-witted, the boor turned into the perfect gentleman, the stinker transformed himself into the elegant dandy, the sloucher smartened up, the decrepit recaptured his lost youth, the godly gone wild, the self-respecting kicked over the traces, all this because of love!"[19] Ibn Hazm has gotten it exactly right. Love pushes you to go beyond your usual routine and into directions you might not otherwise have taken. Which brings us back to our list. Many of the sixty words describe love as a compelling voyage (*huyam*), a step into the unknown (*ghamarat*), an adventure in alien territories. And if such an adventure is risky for the average person, it was even more so for the caliphs, which is why Harun Ar-Rachid never left pleasure to chance. It had to be planned for, strategized, and integrated into the calendar.

To be able to enter into the world of emotions and sexual attraction without looking silly or becoming embarrassed, one has to make pleasure a sacred priority and allocate time for it, just as one would with a religious festival. To put pleasure on the sacred calendar does not mean squeezing two days of relaxation into a hectic two-week-long business trip. No, it means just the opposite: switching priorities and putting what may be weeks of relaxation on the calendar first, and then adding the business trip. At least this is what I learned from reading about how Harun Ar-Rachid planned for his *"majliss,"* or *"time for pleasure."* He planned for them exactly as he planned for battle and sacred pilgrimages to Mecca.

---

1. The first year of the Muslim calendar corresponds to the year 622 of the Christian calendar, and commemorates the prophet Mohammed's migration from Mecca (his hometown, which was then ferociously pagan and rejected his monotheist religion) to Medina, where he started ruling over the first Muslim community. Immediately after the death of the Prophet, there was a short period of three decades (from the year 11 to the year 41) where four caliphs identified as orthodox *(rachidun)* ruled over the Muslims. Then, Muawiya, the first Umayyad, took control in 661 (the year 41 of the Islamic calendar) and created a dynasty, by announcing that his son would inherit his throne.

2. There were twenty-eight Umayyad caliphs if we discount the branch of the dynasty that ruled Spain (from 756 to 1042 A.D.) and thirty-seven Abbasid caliphs.

3. Jalalu'ddin As-suyuti, *History of the Caliphs,* translated from the original Arabic by H. S. Jarrett (Amsterdam: Oriental Press, 1970), p. 291. The author As-suyuti lived in the fifteenth century.

4. Mas'udi, English translation of his "Turiy Ad-dahab," *The Meadows of Gold, The Abbassids,* by Paul Lunde and Caroline Stone (New York: Kegan Paul International, 1989), p. 389. Mas'udi was born in 896 and died in 956.

5. Mas'udi, ibid.

6. Jalalu'ddin As-suyuti, op. cit., p. 297.

7. Jalalu'ddin As-suyuti, op. cit., p. 297.

8. Al-Isbabani, "Aghani" (volume 17, pp. 44–46, edition Bulaq, 1225), translated by Bernard Lewis in *Islam* (New York: Harper and Row, 1974), vol. l, pp. 26 and 28.

9. Ibid.

10. Ibn Khalikhan, *Wafayat al A'yan,* biographie de Zubeida No 242, vol. II, p. 314.

11. Mas'udi, op. cit., p. 390.

12. Kitab al Aghani, vol. 9, p. 88, mentioned in Ahmed Amin, *Doha al Islam* (Cairo: Maktabat an-nahda, 1961), vol. I, p. 9.

13. Ibn as-Sai, *Nissaa' al Khulafa',* op. cit., p. 85.

14. Ibid.

15. George Dimitri Sawa, "Music Performance Practice in Early Abbassid Era 132–320 A.H./750–932 A.D." (Toronto: Pontifical Institute of Medieval Studies, 1989), pp. 6 and 7.

16. "L'Exigence d'aimer," interview of Jamal Eddine Bencheikh by Fethi Benslama and Thierry Fabre in *Qantara* Magazine de l'Institut du Monde Arabe. Paris. Special issue "De l'Amour et des Arabes." (On Love and the Arabs). N° 18, Janvier, Février, Paris, 1996. p. 23.

17. Jalalu'ddin As-suyuti, *History of the Caliphs,* op. cit., p. 338.

18. Jalalu'ddin As-suyuti, op. cit., p. 339.

19. Ibn Hazm al Andaloussi, *Tawq al Hamama: fi al alfati wa alullaf* (Beirut: manchourate dar maktabat al hayat, 1972). The English translation is that of A. J. Abberry, *The Ring of the Dove* (London: Luzac and Co., 1935), p. 35.

# 9

# The Majliss: Pleasure as Sacred Ritual

You can't experience strong sensuous involvement if you keep looking at your watch every ten minutes; that is the lesson I learned from reading medieval history books about Harun Ar-Rachid. A Muslim caliph's duty is to aim for the *al wassat,* the ideal middle between two extremes—between earthly temptations and celestial aspirations, life and death, pleasure and war. And so, the perfect *majliss* must unfold, like a well-planned battle, according to a prescribed scenario wherein the actors and the terrain, as well as the provisions, are carefully determined in advance.

The word *majliss* comes from the verb *jalasa,* which means to sit down with the idea of relaxing motionless for some time, for the sake of pure enjoyment. The word *majliss* means a group of people with similar interests who meet in an attractive place, such as a garden or a terrace, for the sheer pleasure of conversing together and having a good time. "The musical *majliss* meant an assembly of people listening to music performances and competitions," explains writer George Dimitri Sawa, who has devoted a whole book to the subject. People come to enjoy learning from listening to one another and contribute to "discussions and debates on music, history, theory, criticism, and aesthetics."[1]

During the caliphs' time, the indoor *majliss* "took place in superbly decorated rooms. Floors and walls were made of marble or were covered with silk brocade embroidered with gold thread. The caliph's raised throne was adorned with a variety of precious stones, while along the walls to the left and right of the throne were couches with ebony frames for the audience and the musicians."[2] Wine and the mixing of the sexes heightened the sensuality of the *majliss*, which when they were especially successful lasted all day and all night.

Now, when it comes to the drinking of wine, Islam forbids it (Sura 5:91). However, Muslims are just like Christians, Jews, and Buddhists—they know what is proscribed as sinful, but do not necessarily always obey the sacred prescriptions, or else they would be angels. And precisely because wine is forbidden, it is linked in the Muslim psyche to pleasure as a revenge against decay and the fleeting hours pushing us irreversibly toward death. Since antiquity, Muslim countries such as Algeria, Morocco, and Tunisia have been known for their production of delicious wines, which was one reason the Romans occupied that part of the world for centuries. Archeological missions operating in the Mediterranean today often bring to the surface Roman shipwrecks that had foundered while transporting North African wine and olive oil. Also, many historical records refer frequently to the drinking of wine in hedonistically in-clined Berber Morocco, especially in Badis and other Mediterranean cities of the north. Reported Mohamed al Ouazzane, also known as Leo Africanus, in his sixteenth-century memoir: "Badis is a small city on the Mediter-ranean . . . its population is divided into two groups, the fishermen and the pirates who go in their boats to raid the Christian coasts. . . . There is an important street in the city inhabited by the Jews where one could buy wine consid-ered delicious by most of the inhabitants. The people of this city go almost daily, whenever the weather is fine, on their boats and enjoy themselves drinking and singing in the midst of the sea."[3]

Also in the sixteenth century, at least one Muslim em-peror, Jahangir, the ruler of India, was known to be a heavy drinker. As for the poet Omar Khayyam, whose verses are still sung by many in the Muslim world today, he devoted most of his poetry to a celebration of wine as an extreme hedonistic pleasure—with a rather morbid undercurrent. In his poetry, the pleasure derived from wine makes one aware of the passage of time and the fleeting charms of our

strictly numbered days. This philosophical connection between wine, fleeting happiness, and decay explains why
Khayyam's poetry is still sung today, both by those who
drink and those who do not:

> Let not sorrow wither the joyful heart
> Nor stones of affliction wear away your season of
>     happiness.
> Nobody knows the hidden future—
> Wine, a lover, and enjoying the heart's desire all you
>     need.
> Short measures are best of everything except wine
> And wine is best from the hand of courtly beauties. . . .[4]

Even today, in many of the Muslim countries along the
sunny Mediterranean, the local demand for wine is so consistent that rising prices due to increased taxes do not seem
to affect sales. But what about the ancient Muslim rulers,
one might wonder—did they drink? Well, since many of
their lives are described in great detail by historians, we do
know that many Arab caliphs, Turkish sultans, and Mughal
emperors enjoyed their wine. What is unusual about the
Arab rulers is that they usually hid their fun behind the
*hijab,* which literally means "veil." According to Jahiz, my
favorite, witty ninth-century writer who frequented the
Abbasid court, caliphs in general, including Harun Ar-
Rachid, sat behind the veil when drinking. "If someone says

he has seen Ar-Rachid drinking anything but water, be sure he is lying," wrote Jahiz. "Only his favorite *jarya* witnessed his wine-drinking. Sometimes, when a song moved him, he will display his joy, but without exaggeration."[5]

The *majliss* ceremonies unfolded according to strict protocol. However, explains Jahiz, talented *jarya,* who competed with male poets and musicians, could subvert the rules quite easily because their talents heightened their sexual attraction. This opened up enormous opportunities for women slaves who came to Baghdad as booty after conquests. By competing in the arts and sciences, they could not only climb the social ladder, but also raise their value in the slave market, and thereby subvert the ruling male hierarchy altogether. Since the slave buyers were by necessity the richest and most powerful men in the Muslim world, a woman could use her intellectual proficiency and professional achievements to narrow the distance between her and the decision-makers.

And here we stumble upon a key, albeit hidden and potentially fatal, trap of the harem: A man in love risks becoming a slave of his *jarya.* Intellectually and professionally competent *jarya* became the rulers of their masters' minds and senses, thus acquiring an enormous influence that was completely divorced from their capacity to bear children—the only ability that gave slave women legal status (known as *Umm walad,* or mother of a child). Seduction of the master through an intense physical and intellectual exchange was considered to give him exquisite pleasure. "This kind of *jarya* offers the man a scale of pleasures which are rarely combined," explains Jahiz, who was reputed to be both physically ugly and extremely interested in decoding the magic of attraction, "because many senses are involved at once" in "one of the most irresistible and dangerous kinds of seductions."[6]

During this era, the conflict between the sexes was in a way managed like the conflict between cultures. Though loaded with antagonisms, it enriched whoever dared to engage in it. To fall in love is to experiment with the different, to open oneself up to the risky pleasures of unfamiliar sensations and emotions, in a place where fear and the desire for discovery are fatally connected. To take part, one needs two precious assets: a lot of free time to invest in the relationship and the courage to become vulnerable. Men of the era who wished to engage in an erotic exchange with a talented woman had to learn to write poetry, to put feelings into rhythmic words. Harun Ar-Rachid's poetry was decidedly second-rate, but the surprising thing about him is that he did not feel ridiculous trying.

Harun Ar-Rachid was a man who used what Roland Barthes calls "the sensuous charge of words": "Language is a skin: I rub my language against the other. It is as if I had words instead of fingers, or fingers at the tip of my words."[7] Although Harun Ar-Rachid had thousands of *jarya* and often fell in love, he could get emotionally entangled with only one woman at a time. Only once did the brave caliph get emotionally tied up with three beauties simultaneously and the result was particularly lousy poetry.

The names of Harun's three beauties were: Sihr, which means "Magic"; Diya, which means "Radiance"; and Khunt, which means "Femininity." And here is the elaborate result of the caliph's attempt to rub languages with three ravishing creatures at the same time:

Sihr, Diya, and Khunt are *sihr, diya,* and *khunt*
The first stole one third of my heart and the others
    ran away with the rest . . .
The three ladies lead me by the bridle,
and manage to occupy every single inch of my
    heart . . .
Is not that strange that the entire planet obeys me,
and I obey these ladies who are precisely set on
    rebelling against me.
All this is due to the power of love,
which grants them a mightier sway than the
    supremacy I have.[8]

Once the caliph had finished writing down these words, he asked a musician to put them to music and sing them at the next *majliss*. But since Harun much preferred listening to talented *jarya,* who were professional wordsmiths, I suspect that he knew his limitations and had no illusions about his talent as a poet. Instead, he focused on being attractive and stocked up on thousands of shirts and robes. When the list of what he owned became public after his death, Muslim believers must have been baffled by their prince's extravagant taste. Writes Al Fadl Ibn al-Rabi:

When Muhammad al Amin succeeded his father Harun al Rachid as Caliph in the year 193 (A.D. 809), he ordered me to count the clothing, furnishings, vessels and equipment in the stores. I summoned the secretaries and store-keepers and continued counting for months, during which I inspected treasures which I did not dream the caliphal stores contained. . . . The list of contents was as follows: "4,000 embroidered robes, 4,000 silk cloaks lined with sable, mink, and other furs, 10,000 shirts and shifts, 10,000 caftans, 4,000 Turbans, . . . 1,000 hoods . . . 1,000 capes of various kinds . . . , 1,000 precious china vessels . . . , many kinds of perfume . . . , 1,000 jeweled rings . . . , 1,500 silk carpets . . . , 1,000 silk cushions and pillows . . . , 1,000 washbasins . . . , 1,000 ewers . . . , 1,000 belts, 10,000 decorated swords, 150,000 lances, 100,000 bows, 1,000 special suits of armor, 50,000 common suits of armor, 10,000 helmets, 150,000 shields, 4,000 pairs of half boots, most of them lined with sable, mink, and other kind of furs, with a knife and a kerchief in each half-boot, 4,000 pairs of socks, 4,000 small tents with their appurtenances."[9]

To appreciate how far our caliph had gone in violating the rules of austerity that his dynasty was supposed to abide by, one has to remember that the Abbasids avoided luxurious attire and stuck to one basic color—black. "It has been the tradition for the caliph," explains one tenth-century expert, "to sit on an elevated seat on a throne covered with pure Armenian silk, or with silk and wool. . . . The caliph wears a long-sleeved garment, dyed black, the outer garment is either plain or embroidered with white silk or wool. He does not, however, wear sigillatum (patterned) silk brocade or decorated garments."[10] Without a doubt, as Imam Ibn al-Jawzi said, the hardest of all struggles for a Muslim leader is not against the Christian enemy, but against his own passions. Even the Prophet Mohammed, in one of his *hadiths* (sayings reported by his disciples after his death), according to Ibn al-Jawzi, identified resisting one's passions as being "the big *jihad*" (*al jihad al akbar*), and fighting the enemy as being only "the small *jihad*" (*al jihad al asghar*).[11]

Harun Ar-Rachid seems to have been much more successful in waging the small *jihad* than he was in the big one. One time, when he was brooding about whether to purchase 'Inane, a famous attractive poetess whose price was very high, Asma'i, one of his close companions, asked what was bothering him. The caliph confessed that it was 'Inane who was giving him trouble, but added, "It is only her poetry which attracts me to her." Asma'i then tried to tell the caliph, as politely as he could, that he did not believe a word he'd said. "Sure, there is nothing to be attracted to in 'Inane but her poetry, Sire," he said. "Would the Commander of the Faithful have been enchanted to have sexual intercourse with al Farazdaq for example?" At that, "Harun Ar-Rachid burst into such a deep laughter that his head went backward."[12] Farazdaq was a famous but extremely coarse male poet who excelled in describing battle scenes.

For a caliph, chanting poetry or playing chess with an attractive *jarya* was not like engaging in the same activities with a man. Of course, the caliph was free to choose a male partner if he liked, and homosexuality was quite acceptable in the multicultural, cosmopolitan, and tolerant Abbasid court. Sexual preference was regarded as just one more difference between people. You could choose to either keep to your own sex or venture to open yourself up to the unknown. One of the most sophisticated and wittiest stars of the Abbasid court was the Persian poet Abu Nuwas, who read fiery verses extolling young men's beauty. But even he was sometimes taken in by a woman's wit and dazzling intelligence and was known to have had affairs with exceptional *jarya* from time to time.

The overriding message one gets from reading the twenty-four volumes of *The Book of Songs* (*Kitab al Aghani*), which records in extraordinary detail how the caliphs enjoyed themselves, is that homosexuality did not carry with it the dangers that heterosexuality did. A heterosexual encounter implied taking much greater risks because one had to confront the foreign and embrace the different "other." Incidentally, the Arabic language is rich with words for sexually attractive handsome young men, such as *ghulam,* which literally means "page," that carry clear homosexual connotations; while in the West, even the term "homosexuality" was not commonly used until the 1880s. And then, it was used only by medical doctors and psychiatrists who referred to it as a sickness.[13]

But to get back to the Abbasid court, a heterosexual encounter was regarded as an adventure, a door leading into the unknown. A man needed a certain amount of heroic courage if he was to challenge his familiar self and jump into a passionate love affair with that most unpredictable of all strangers—a woman. A woman who was by definition also an enemy, since the harem had turned her into a prisoner.

The story of the *Ghulamiat,* or page girls, is quite revealing of this idea, which seems so strange to us today—that one needs special courage to engage in heterosexual involvement. When Princess Zubaida discovered that her son Amin, whom she hoped would become heir to the throne, had homosexual tendencies, she was sure she could "cure" him by dressing attractive girls like *Ghulam,* as young slave-boys. In so doing, she launched a whole new fashion in Baghdad: "Zubaida chose young girls remarkable for the elegance of their figures and the charm of their faces," writes Mas'udi, the ninth-century historian. "She had them wear turbans and gave them clothes woven and embroidered in the royal factories, and had them fix their hair with fringes and love locks and drew it back at the nape of the neck after the fashion of young men. She dressed them in close-fitting, wide-sleeved robes called *qaba* and wide belts which showed off their waists and their curves. Then she sent them to her son Amin. As they filed into his presence, he was enchanted. He was captivated by their looks and appeared with them in public. It was then that the fashion for having young slave girls with short hair, wearing *qaba* and belts, became established at all levels of society. They were called page-girls (*ghulamiat*)."[14] The *"ghulamiat"* were the Arab equivalent of the European *"Les Garçonnes,"* fashionable women who dressed like men in the 1920s.

By the ninth century, Baghdad had become openly tolerant toward the foreign cultures of former enemies such as the Romans and the Persians. This new acceptance brought wealth and glory to the Arabs, who, up until the advent of Islam, had lived as marginal nomads in the Arabian desert. However, tolerance and cross-fertilization did not mean absence of conflict. Abbasid courts were torn by strong rivalries between Persians and Arabs (which are still so evident in the Middle East today—remember the 1980s Iran-Iraq

War). And the conflict between the sexes was equally dangerous, especially when attraction came into play. Locking up thousands of women in harems was a drastic measure taken by caliphs who wished to minimize risk by making rejection impossible. If a woman did not care for her master, she could not slam the door and leave. But even within the harem's supposedly safe walls, the caliph had to take risks by expressing his emotions. Which brings us back to the Western men's harem.

What happens to a man's emotions when female beauty is an image—and that image is fabricated by the man himself?

What happens to emotions when we turn away from Harun Ar-Rachid's harem, where the caliph got entangled in intense erotic exchanges involving all his senses, to the painted harems of Ingres and Matisse or the filmed harems of Hollywood? How can a man get involved with a real woman—his wife or lover—when at the same time he is involved with a painted or filmed image?

It was at this point that I decided to revisit that most glorious, influential, and invincible of European harems—the one created by Jean-Auguste-Dominique Ingres. Reproduced on thousands and thousands of book covers, CDs, and magazines all over the West, his harem may date back to the nineteenth century, but is more present than ever in our digital age.

If I could infiltrate Ingres's harem, I thought, I might be able to understand some of the mysterious secrets of Western men's psyche, as well as their emotional and erotic landscape. If I knew more about Western men's feelings toward women, I might have fewer quarrels with Kemal. He was constantly telling me, whenever I raised my voice in Chateaubriand, the restaurant near the university where we and our colleagues flocked for couscous in the afternoon, "Fatema, I am always amazed by how much you know about Arab history and the Abbasids, and how little you know about me." This kind of sentence would break my heart. I would feel guilty, apologize, and try to reach for Kemal's hand, but he always stopped my self-flagellation by reminding me that, like most Moroccans, he did not appreciate couples touching each other in public. "Please, Fatema, restrain yourself," he would say. "Have you not seen the Dean of the University sitting on your left, and our Mullah-like conservative Benkiki on your right?"

I desperately needed to increase my knowledge of men and their enigmatic reactions. It shocked me to realize that, even after so many decades of trying to understand Kemal, I still managed to drive him so crazy sometimes that he stopped seeing me for weeks or even months. Of course, on those occasions, I always mobilized the entire university population to intervene on my behalf and help me win his forgiveness, but it still took time for things to get back to normal. Understanding how a man's mind and emotions work is definitely not an easy task for a woman. I have managed to learn new skills in my life, like mastering foreign languages and using a computer, but when it comes to figuring out how men's emotions work, I have not advanced much.

But to get back to my harem obsession: What happens to shifting boundaries and unstable privileges when the filmed or painted harem image is introduced as a strategic component of sexual dynamics? Could it be that Ingres's odalisques were a kind of shield to protect him from his own emotions? I could not wait to get back into Monsieur Ingres's world.

---

1. George Dimitri Sawa, *Music Performance Practice in Early 'Abbassid Era* (Toronto: Pontifical Institute of Medieval Studies, 1989), op. cit., p. 20.

2. Ibid.

3. My translation from the Arabic version of *Description of Africa,* translated from the French by M. Hijji and M. Lakhdar (Rabat: al Jami'a al Maghribiya li ta'lif wa tarjama, 1980), p. 234.

4. *The Ruba'iyat of Omar Khayyam,* translated by Peter Avery and John Heath-Stubbs (New York: Penguin Books, 1979), p. 108.

5. al-Jahiz, *Kitab at-Taj: Fi akhlaq al muluk (The Book of the Crown: Behavior of Kings)* (Beirut: Ach-charika al lubnaniya lil-kitab, 1970), p. 44. Jahiz died in 276 hijira, or A.D. 889. For a French translation of this essay, see Charles Pellat, "Le Livre de La Couronne," Société d'Editions (Paris: Les Belles Lettres, 1954), p. 65.

6. al-Jahiz, op. cit., p. 65.

7. Roland Barthes, *A Lover's Discourse: Fragments,* translated from the French by Richard Howard (New York: Hill and Wang, 1978), p. 73.

8. My translation of the original, from the famous *Book of Songs (Kitab al Aghani)* by Abi l-Faraj al-Isbahani. The quote is in vol. 16, p. 345.

9. Bernard Lewis, *Islam,* translated from Arabic (New York: Harper and Row, 1974), vol. II, p. 140.

10. Hilal Ibn Sabi', *Rusum Dar al Khilafa (Rules and Regulations of the 'Abbasid Court),* translated from Arabic by Elie A. Salem (Beirut: American University of Beirut, 1977), p. 73.

11. Quoted by Imam Ibn al-Jawzi, *Kitab dammu l-hawa*, publisher not identified, 1962. The author lived in the twelfth century.

12. Al-Asbahani, *Al Imaa Ach-chawair (Slave-Girl Poets)*, op. cit., p. 41.

13. "Mais des médecins commencent à parler de l'homosexualité (le mot n'est guère utilisé couramment par eux qu'à partir des années 1880) comme d'une perversion à soigner et non plus d'un vice à punir. C'est là un progrés important puisque l' 'inverti' n'est alors plus justiciable des tribunvaux correctionnels mais des cabinets médicaux. A Vienne, Krafft-Ebing, l'un des maîtres de Freud, publie sa 'Psychopathia sexualis' où il étude longuement, au titre de la 'sexualité antipathique' 'les sentiments homosexuels dans les deux sexes.' " Odon Vallet, *L'Affaire Wilde,* collection Folio (Paris: Gallimard, 1995), p. 30.

14. Mas'udi, *Meadows of Gold,* op. cit., pp. 390–391.

# 10

# In the Intimacy of a European Harem: Monsieur Ingres

ow did Monsieur Ingres manage to have a real Christian wife, whom he married in front of a priest, and at the same time officially paint and sell nude odalisques? Did his wife get jealous when he gazed for hours at the buttocks and thighs of *La Grande Odalisque?* As an Arab woman, I would have been watching him very carefully, just as the *jarya* had watched Harun Ar-Rachid in his harem, where jealousies flared and burned many lives. Was Monsieur Ingres in love with his wife or was theirs an unromantic *mariage de raison,* an arranged marriage? Was he a wildly passionate man, so hot and sexy that Madame Ingres could not cope with his lustful cravings and so accepted the fact that he painted nude images to calm himself? This could be an explanation for the presence of the mysterious Turkish odalisques in a republican French household. It is similar to the explanation frequently given in my hometown of Fez, whenever a middle-aged wife looks for a young bride to help her satisfy her husband's virile demands. Or, at least, those virile demands are often the *official* explanation provided. The real reason is usually economic: In a country where polygamy is enforced by men as sacred law, the aging wife volunteers to find her husband a second bride in order to be able to stick around. The wife swallows her pride and controls her jealousy as she tries to create a new role for herself—that of the removed, but dignified, asexual, menopausal first wife. Without the security of a salary or second income, to express jealousy when your aging husband is ogling younger women is to risk embarking on a penniless future.

Jealousy is so demeaning, as we all know. When I am jealous, it is the only time I can understand how easy it would be to become a criminal. Often, the Muslim woman who chooses to swallow her jealousy turns to religion as a substitute and creates for herself a spiritual life by regularly attending the mosque and religious celebrations. This, after all, is the "Orient," where injustice against women is still camouflaged as sacred law. But when a modern Muslim woman has a salary, like myself, the jealous fights that rage in Muslim kingdoms are similar to those that rage in the republics. Many of my male university colleagues complain about jealous wives and girlfriends who slice their car tires so badly that the gentlemen think twice before upsetting them again. And Madame Ingres was freed from the priests and their manipulations thanks to the French Revolution, wasn't she? Did she really enjoy witnessing her beloved husband dreaming so openly about exotic rivals? Did Monsieur and Madame Ingres have a stormy marriage? Did she scream at him to stop him from painting odalisques? Or shove him down onto her couch and ravish him? I would have buried the damn brushes or given them away to needy painters. How do the French deal with emotions? Does the French Declaration of the Rights of Man and Citizen say anything at all about jealousy?

Ingres was nine years old in 1789, the year in which the French people established *"Liberté, Égalité, Fraternité"* as the foundation of the Republic of France. And Ingres was a true son of the ideals of the French Revolution: Born in modest circumstances, he then rose up the social ladder effortlessly, his talent recognized, honored, and splendidly rewarded. But if the Republic changed social conditions and paved the way for children of humble origins to shine professionally and thrive economically, nothing of the sort was guaranteed in the more shadowy fields of romance and emotional fulfillment.

Ingres's public life unfolds like a magnificent advertisement for the French Republic. But the Revolution did not seem to have made the successful young man any bolder emotionally. He was not able to take the initiative in choosing his own wife, but instead fell back on the traditional arranged marriage. He got engaged twice to young women who attracted him, but for whatever reason, both engagements were broken off.

For me, as an Arab woman extremely preoccupied with human rights, Ingres's life is fascinating. Although he was a liberated Western man fed on democratic ideas, he couldn't choose his own wife and fantasized about slave women as the epitome of beauty. What kind of revolution, I wonder, do we need to make men dream of self-assertive independent women as the epitome of beauty?

The 1789 French Declaration of the Rights of Man and Citizen was a landmark in the history of mankind. In it, subordination of women was rejected as a sign of despotism. Despotism and slavery were both condemned as shameful characteristics of uncivilized Asian nations. "The servitude of women," wrote Montesquieu in *The Spirit of Laws,* "is very much in conformity with the genius of despotic government, which likes to abuse everything. Thus in Asia, domestic servitude and despotic government have been seen to go hand in hand in every age."[1] The writings of Montesquieu, who was born in 1689 and died in 1755, twenty-five years before the birth of Ingres, inspired the French people. And the monstrous Asian despotism that Montesquieu so roundly condemned when defining his cherished democracy was none other than that of the Turkish Ottoman empire.[2] Therefore, one would expect that a painter who celebrated odalisques, or Turkish slaves, as ideal beauties in the early days of the French Republic would have been rejected as an uncivilized savage. But this was not so; not only was Ingres's career successful, but his paintings of odalisques were bought by some of the most influential political figures of his century.

Ingres was born to modest parents in Montauban, a small city in Tarn-et-Garonne. "His father, Jean-Marie-Joseph, had settled in Montauban as a decorative sculptor and rapidly became the artist for every job in the town. . . . In 1777, he married Anne Moulet, the daughter of a master wigmaker at the Court of Aides, by whom he had five children, of which the oldest was Jean-Auguste-Dominique."[3] Montauban was a troubled city during Ingres's childhood, and he lived under the shadow of religious violence. A city afflicted with social unrest is never an advantageous environment for a child, but it is especially unsettling for the firstborn of a large family whose father is an artist with an irregular income.

Although Ingres was born in a secular republic that guaranteed freedom of thought and pushed priests out of the political limelight, religion still had an enormous influence. As a small boy, he was literally immersed in Christian culture, starting with the ritual of baptism. Later, he was sent to a religious school where he surprised his stern instructors by developing "profane" skills in such areas as music and drawing. "First, the child was put in school with the Frères des Écoles Chrétiennes (Brothers of Christian Schools). These monks, troubled by the events and in search of a difficult re-adaptation, taught very little and badly. What knowledge the child acquired was mediocre: too many gaps, great lacks of learning even in the basics. Ingres would regret this for a long time to come. Yet, precocious gifts showed up in him: they took the form of violin and pencil."[4] Music and playing the violin would become the painter's lifelong hobby and he would give the French language a new expression: "Le Violon d'Ingres." This meant, among other things, that a person who has many talents is forced to relinquish some and enjoy them as hobbies only. Nonetheless, Ingres was, according to experts, an excellent musician.

At the age of eleven, Ingres was sent to the Académie de Toulouse, and at age seventeen, his painting abilities were so impressive that he was dispatched to Paris to study in the studio of the great master painter Jacques-Louis David. There, he discovered that his classmates enjoyed an affluence and savoir faire that he lacked. This realization, according to one Ingres biographer, Norman Schlenoff, caused him to develop an enormous shame for his humble origins that he never really overcame. Ingres seldom spoke, for example, about the time that he worked as a busboy in his uncle's café, rinsing glasses, drawing portraits of clients, and playing in impromptu orchestras for neighborhood dances. The young painter would soon take his revenge on his well-to-do classmates, however.

At the age of twenty-one, Ingres received the first Grand Prize of Rome, an honor coveted by every student in David's atelier. The *Grand Prix* would permit him to continue his training at the French Academy in Rome. Money problems did not allow him to actually leave for Rome until five years later, in 1806, but receiving the Prize had another immediate advantage—he was excused from military service. This was not a minor privilege at that time, as Napoleon's army was then transforming the map of Europe and the Mediterranean. In 1798, the French army had invaded Egypt, one of the jewels of the Muslim empire, ruled by Ottoman Sultans. That invasion had shaken the world because up until then, it had been the powerful Ottoman Sultans who were threatening Europe. Ingres had turned eighteen that very year, and especially welcomed being excused from military service because he abhorred the sight of blood and never painted battle scenes, a favorite topic of many artists of his time. For many French artists, to be invited to paint battle scenes or join diplomatic missions was their only chance to travel to exotic lands at the expense of the state. Delacroix, for example, a contemporary of Ingres, was invited to travel to Morocco as part of a diplomatic mission in 1832. And it was during this trip that Delacroix made a detour to Algiers, where he visited the harem that was to inspire his famous *Women of Algiers* painting, re-created in France a few years later from memory, diaries, and sketches.[5]

Although Ingres had not been particularly anxious to accompany diplomatic missions or visit the Orient, this does not seem to have hampered his career in any way. Years later, in 1834, he was named Director of the Académie de France in Rome, and in 1841, when he returned to Paris at the end of his mission, he was triumphantly welcomed; "The Marquis de Pastoret organizes a dinner in his honor with 426 guests followed by a concert conducted by Berlioz. King Louis-Philippe invites him to Versailles and receives him at his home in Neuilly. Commissions for portraits are multiplying."[6] In 1850, he was appointed President of the École des Beaux Arts; in 1855, he received, from the hands of the Emperor himself, the Cross of Grand Officier of the Legion of Honor; and finally in 1862, he was named Senator and given the Médaille d'Or (Gold Medal) by 215 French artists.

But athough Ingres did not meet Napoleon on the battlefield, he could not escape him altogether. In 1803, Ingres received a commission to paint the commander's portrait, as did Greuze, another of the era's most important painters. The two men traveled together to the residence of the First Consul in Liège for a short sitting, but when they arrived, they discovered that they had to work fast, for "the feverishly active Napoleon had little time to pose."[7] To paint Napoleon was the dream of all French painters at that time, and after receiving recognition of such magnitude, Ingres turned to romance and love. He started to look for a bride.

The first two women Ingres loved enough to want to

marry were far from being passive odalisques. The first was Mademoiselle Julie Forestier and she was a painter and musician. Ingres was twenty-six when the engagement was officially announced in June 1806. A few months later, however, the two had to part company because Ingres finally had enough money to go to Rome. In October 1806, he arrived in the Italian city, and for the first time in his life caught a glimpse of the sea, at Ostia, a beautiful spot a few kilometers from Rome. The director of the sumptuous Villa Medicis, where the French Academy was situated, gave him a private studio with a fantastic view of the Pincio.

Once settled in Rome, Ingres did not forget about his fiancée, and sent her father a gift—a painting of a landscape of the Villa Borghese. But one year later, during the summer of 1807, he broke off his engagement and Mademoiselle Forestier hastily returned the painting to him. That very year, as if to compensate for his disappointment, Ingres painted *La Baigneuse à mi-corps,* which depicts a nude seated woman, seen from the back, her arms apparently crossed over her breasts. She is wearing a magnificent silk turban carelessly tied that is so characteristic of many of Ingres's later odalisques, including his famous *Baigneuse de Valpinçon* (Bather of Valpinçon), named after the person who acquired the painting. The bather seen from the back was "Ingres's first great painting of the female nude," writes critic Robert Rosenblum. "[It] creates a world of breathtaking stillness [of] the elusive ideal of timelessness, classical perfection, which periodically haunts Western art."[8] This same mysterious, faceless bather will also haunt Ingres for more than fifty years. She will still occupy center stage in his *Turkish Bath,* which he finished in 1862, when he was an old man past eighty. "Ingres must have realized that with this nude he had achieved a kind of immutable perfection," writes Rosenblum, "For just as he might copy, with variations, the eternal harmonies invented by Raphael, so too was he to re-create his own *Bather of Valpinçon* in a series of more elaborate bathing compositions that culminated with *The Turkish Bath.*"[9]

After his first failure in love, Ingres waited five years before he became engaged again, this time to an exotic Scandinavian woman. He was thirty-two when, in 1812, he wrote to his parents asking for their permission to become engaged to Laura Zoega, the daughter of a Danish archeologist. But this engagement was even shorter than the first, and broken off abruptly.

The following year, Ingres decided to take a much less romantic approach to choosing a companion—he would marry someone he did not know. He turned to the wife of his friend Monsieur Lauréal, a high-ranking official in Rome's French court, and she suggested her cousin Madeleine Chapelle, a thirty-one-year-old *modiste,* or maker of fashionable attire. He corresponded with her, decided to marry her—a woman he had never seen—and asked his friends to schedule an interview. Madeleine came to meet her future husband, and they convened near Nero's tomb outside Rome, on the road to France.

Then, on the fourth of December, 1813, Ingres and Madeleine Chapelle wed. Although not much is known about Ingres's domestic life, one thing appears to be certain: He and Madeleine had a monogamous marriage. However, only a year after their wedding, Ingres introduced a slave woman into his emotional life—his famous *Grande Odalisque*. But citizen Madeleine Ingres did not scream and protest as a Muslim woman would. In my native Fez medina, women staged huge uproars when their husbands married a second wife, holding funeral-like protests, during which their friends and relatives wailed along with them in the harem courtyards. The fact that polygamy is institutionalized by male law does not make it emotionally acceptable to women. Many queens, as historians have written, suffocated or choked their husbands when they discovered their plans to acquire a second wife, or when the rival actually arrived in the home. Still other historical records show that it was often the women who were the victims of jealousy. "A seventeenth-century document in the Topkapi Palace archives," writes Alev Lytle Croutier in her book, *Harem*, "speaks of the rivalry between Sultana Gülnush and the odalisque Gülbeyaz—(Rose-white), which led to a tragic end. Sultan Mehmed IV had been deeply enamored of Gülnush . . . but after Gülbeyaz entered his harem, his affections began to shift. Gülnush, still in love with the sultan, became madly jealous. One day, as Gülbeyaz was sitting on a rock and watching the sea, Gülnush quietly pushed her off the cliff and drowned the young odalisque."[10]

It was 1814 and Ingres had just turned thirty-four. Unlike Madeleine, his French wife, who could walk and talk, and probably had many domestic chores to attend to, *La Grande Odalisque* was created to do nothing but lie around and look beautiful. In effect, by spending months painting a beautiful woman, Ingres was declaring daily to his wife that she was ugly! Or, at least, that is what a Muslim woman would conclude. How men's and women's emotions unfold in a French harem like the one created by Ingres is incomprehensible to me. What was Ingres's emotional problem? Was he afraid to invest too much emotionally in his wife? The emotional landscape is definitely one of the keys to understanding cultural differences between East and West, I realized. Clearly, I could learn much about my own emotional problems if I could understand why Madeleine Ingres was not jealous.

Or was it perhaps that Madeleine Ingres did feel jealous but was afraid to show it? Are Western women who enjoy monogamy discouraged from expressing their jealousy as a price for that privilege? With that thought, I rushed over to the huge bookstore in the Louvre basement, bought more books on Ingres, and sat in a sunny café on the rue de Rivoli to scavenge for information about Madeleine Ingres.

What I found was scanty, but I did learn that historians know enough about Ingres's private life to conclude that the couple shared delightful moments. Financially, Ingres was quite well off and was regarded as one of the "top twelve most privileged artists of the French Republic."[11] He was generous and entertained often and quite lavishly. He also enjoyed going to the opera and had a tendency to stuff himself with pastry. Furthermore, he took real pleasure in posing in the nude, a practice that he'd started as a young artist in David's atelier, where students traditionally posed for one another; "there has survived a copy of a student drawing of Ingres posing in the nude, short and somewhat stout, but striding vigorously forward holding an elegant bow."[12] Later, "a willingness to strip in order to further the cause of art stayed with him. . . . He posed nude as the Virgin Mary for his own painting *The Vow of Louis XIII,* persuading a friend to sketch him as he worked out the position of the legs."[13] And around 1840, when Ingres was nearly sixty, he "began running around the room in a state of undress before throwing himself, panting, onto a mattress."[14] He was described then by a contemporary as "a little man obese and squat . . . without the fear of appearing comic. . . ."[15]

When moved, Ingres expressed his emotions—especially tenderness. He did not hesitate, for example, to write a letter to Madeleine saying how much he missed her presence during the ceremony when Charles X awarded him the Légion d'Honneur in 1824. "When my name was pronounced in the midst of the cheers," he went on, "my poor legs and my face must have given away the state of extreme vulnerability I felt when I had to cover the distance separating me from the king to receive the *Croix* (cross) he gracefully bestowed on me. . . ."[16] Ingres also confessed to Madeleine that he had cried; "You would have cried too if you were there, just like I am still doing while writing to you about it." Ingres was then forty-five and, unlike those men who grow more narcissistic with success, he seems to have mellowed and grown appreciative of the tenderness and emotion he felt toward Madeleine. During this period, he once advised a husband, posing for him for a portrait, to look at his wife so "that his eyes soften."[17] Ingres's fascination with women's emotions, and his attempts to capture their fleeting moods and changing fashions, also contributed to his portraits' appeal.

So it was no wonder that Ingres was devastated when Madeleine, his confidante for more than thirty-five years, died in 1849. Then nearly sixty-nine, he felt so lonely that he decided to remarry three years later. Again he asked friends, this time the Marcottes, to help him arrange his new marriage, and on the 15th of April, 1852, he wed Delphine Ramel. At age forty-two, the new bride was almost thirty years younger than him—a point he often reminded her of—and belonged to a comfortable middle-class family. Before their marriage, she had lived with her father, a mortgage administrator in Versailles.

This second marriage seems to have been as happy as the first. Wrote Ingres to a friend in 1854: "I see nobody or rarely a few friends who have the kindness to admire my present life. My excellent wife is adjusting very well to this way of living. She creates solitude for me and embellishes it almost every evening with two sonatas by the divine Haydn which she interprets very well and with true feeling. Sometimes I accompany her."[18]

Yet, in the midst of this conjugal bliss, Ingres began to paint *The Turkish Bath,* one of his most diabolically voluptuous harems, filled with nude women. The year was 1859, and this time, with the younger Delphine at his side, he seems to have been more emboldened than before as far as his harem fantasies were concerned. Instead of introducing one single odalisque into his monogamous marriage, as he had with Madeleine, he now introduced more than twenty Turkish women, only one of whom looked like Delphine. "The Turkish bath resembles a world both real and imaginary, an erotic fantasy crystallized within the distorting lens of a convex mirror . . . ," writes critic Robert Rosenbaum. "In the head of the nude leaning against the pillow in the right foreground, the plump features of Ingres's new wife, Delphine Ramel, may be recognized."[19]

It took Ingres more than three years to finish his *Turkish*

*Bath,* considered by Edward Lucie-Smith, the author of *Sexuality in Western Art,* as a "particularly complex kind" of image-anchored eroticism.[20] According to him, *The Turkish Bath* is "a hymn to the glory of the omnipresent feminine body—there are nudes everywhere we look; they fill the whole picture-space as if the artist suffered from horror-vacui. . . . These women are animals, herded together and preparing themselves for the pleasure of the male (whom in any case they cannot refuse to satisfy). Secondly, the implications are strongly voyeuristic: we are looking in at a scene normally forbidden to the male gaze."[21]

At least one Frenchwoman, Princess Clotilde, the wife of Prince Napoleon, got extremely jealous of *The Turkish Bath.* Shocked by so much nudity, she forced her husband to get rid of the painting. He gave it back to Ingres, who did not waste a minute before repainting the canvas. "The artist then transformed the painting en tondo and to that end diminished it by a vertical strip and enlarged it on the left with another strip. The transformation was important for in this way a large part of the nude woman in the foreground to the right had disappeared and the pose of her neighbor had changed. Then he added the set table in the foreground, the bather seated on the edge of the basin, and all the figures in the back above her. Then the drapery was cut out. . . ."[22]

And who bought the now-changed painting that every French husband was hesitant to acquire? A Turk! A Muslim man. "In 1864, the work was still in Ingres's studio; it was bought a little later (20,000 francs) by Khalil Bey, the Turkish ambassador in Paris."[23] But four years later, in 1868, the ambassador sold the painting to a French buyer, who sold it again, and it was not until 1911 that it became a possession of the Louvre. Why, I wondered, had Ambassador Khalil Bey gotten rid of the painting? Had his wife nagged him, or had he simply felt a pressing need for French francs? Perhaps, like other Turks of his epoch, he was totally bored with harems; as was mentioned earlier (chap. 7), Turkey in the 1860s was in the midst of one of the most important cultural revolutions to shake despotic Islam. Despotism and the corrupt rule of the Ottoman sultans were being blamed for the sweeping advance of Western colonization, best symbolized by the occupation of Algeria by French troops in 1830. Algeria had been an Ottoman colony, and its occupation fueled a nationalism that took the form of radical reformist movements. Most notable among them was the "Young Turks," who blamed despotic institutions, starting with the harem, as the cause of the Muslim military defeats. The Young Turks promoted the first state-run girls' schools in the 1860s, and four decades later, in 1909, banned the harem altogether, while encouraging women to enter the professions. Could it be that Ambassador Khalil Bey was in some way embarrassed to own an expensive "Parisian harem," and sold it in order to appear "politically correct" on the home front? That is the kind of question I ought to ask my colleague Benkiki back in Rabat. Like all fundamentalists, Benkiki hates the Young Turks, especially their leader Kemal Ataturk, and therefore knows a great deal about Turkey's Revolution, which culminated in the 1920s, when Turkey was declared a republic and Kemal Ataturk became its first president. The abolition of the Caliphate (the office of the Caliph) was declared official in 1924.

The influence of the Turkish Revolution reverberated throughout the Muslim world. Thanks to it, the first schools for girls were established in Morocco—schools that I attended in the 1940s and without which I would have been a desperately frustrated illiterate. I often wonder what I would have done had I been raised illiterate. What comes to my mind most frequently is clairvoyance. Yes, I would have become the best clairvoyant in all the Kingdom of Morocco. Why? Because clairvoyants sell hope and build self-confidence by insisting on their clients' capacity to change the situation in which they find themselves. Hope is what women need to make sense of their senseless lives. Yes, I would have peddled hope. Hope is my drug and official addiction. Pessimism is the luxury of the powerful. I can't afford it.

The enigma of all this is that no trace of the incredible feminist transformation first of Turkey and later of other Muslim countries was to be found in Western paintings. In the 1930s, when Matisse was painting his passive odalisques, Turkish magazines were reproducing photographs of

armed female Ankara University students in military uni-
forms. Sabiha Gokçen, the first Turkish woman pilot, was
pictured flying planes in 1930, while Sureya Agoaglu, a
lawyer, was appearing in the Turkish courts to defend her
clients throughout the 1930s.[24] A wealthy Turk like Khalil
Bey had to migrate to Paris to find harems for sale.

All the harem women that Ingres fantasized about and
painted nonstop for fifty years were idle, helplessly passive,
and always pictured indoors, reclining on sofas in an em-
barrassingly vulnerable nudity. Yet this fantasy of passive
harem women does not exist in the Orient!

Ironically, in the Orient—land of harems, polygamy,
and veils—Muslim men have always fantasized, in both
literature and painting, about self-assertive, strong-
minded, uncontrollable, and mobile women. The Arabs
fantasized about Scheherazade of *The Thousand and One
Nights;* the Persians painted adventurous princesses like
Shirin, who hunted wild animals across continents on
horseback; and the Mughals, or Turco-Mongols, from
central Asia, gave the Muslim world wonderful erotic
paintings filled with strong, independent-looking women
and fragile, insecure-looking men. No wonder that in a
rapidly modernizing Turkey, photographs of women flying planes or manning guns were constantly reproduced
in magazines.

What kind of women haunt Muslim artists' fantasies? What
kind of women did they paint when dreaming of beauties?

These were the questions Claire and Jacques wanted me to answer after I exhausted them raving about Ingres and his incomprehensible emotions.

---

1. Montesquieu, *The Spirit of Laws* (*De l'Esprit Des Lois*), translated and edited by Anne M. Cohler, Basia Carolyn Miller, and Harold Samuel Stone (Cambridge: Cambridge University Press, 1989), p. 270.

2. See Alain Grosrichard's introductory chapter to his book *The Sultan's Court: European Fantasies of the East* (New York: Verso, 1997).

3. Daniel Ternois (Introduction) and Ettore Camesasca (text), *Ingres,* translated from the Italian into French by Simone Darses (Paris: Flammarion, 1984), p. 83. The translation from French to English is my own.

4. Pierre Angrand, *Monsieur Ingres et son Epoque* (Lausanne–Paris: Bibliotheque des Arts, 1967), op. cit., p. 9.

5. "The mission finally left Tangiers in June and, after putting in at Oran, disembarked in Algiers on the 25th of the same month. During this three day stay, Delacroix seems to have been able to arrange a visit to the harem of the dey's reis. From this came one of the most famous of all Orientalist paintings, Women of Algiers in their Quarters (Musée du Louvre, Paris). Delacroix remained haunted by his African journey. Using his sketches and notes, he painted the scenes he had witnessed." From *The Orientalists: Painter-Travellers,* by Lynn Thornton (Paris: ACR edition, Poche Couleur, 1994), pp. 68–69.

6. Ternois and Camesasca, op. cit., p. 85.

7. Robert Rosenblum, *Ingres* (New York: Harry N. Abrams, 1990), p. 52.

8. Rosenblum, *Ingres,* op. cit., p. 66.

9. Rosenblum, *Ingres,* op. cit., p. 66.

10. Alev Lytle Croutier, *Harem* (New York: Abbeville Press, 1998), op. cit., pp. 34–35.

11. Angrand, op. cit., p. 217.

12. James Fenton, "The Zincsmith of Genius," *New York Review of Books,* May 20, 1999, pp. 21–28. The quote is from page 21.

13. Ibid., p. 21.

14. Ibid.

15. Ibid.

16. H. Lapauze, "Le Roman d'Amour de Mr Ingres," Paris, 1910, pp. 282–287, quoted by Pierre Angrand, op. cit., footnote number 2, p. 48.

17. The portrait was that of Cavé. In Pierre Angrand, *La Vie de Mr Ingres*, op. cit., p. 211, footnote number 2.

18. Letter to Pauline Guibert, dated 6 September 1854, quoted in Angrand, p. 247.

19. Rosenblum, *Ingres,* op. cit., p. 128.

20. Edward Lucie-Smith, *Sexuality in Western Art* (London: Thames and Hudson, 1972), p. 180.

21. Ibid.

22. Ternois and Camesasca, op. cit., 118.

23. Ternois and Camesasca, ibid.

24. Sarah Graham-Brown, *Images of Women: Portrayal of Women in Photography of the Middle East 1860–1950* (New York: Columbia University Press, 1988).

# II

# Aggressive Shirin Hunts for Love

Who are the women painted by Muslim men in miniatures? Are they fictional characters, legendary figures, or real queens and princesses? Is there a tradition of painting in Islam? Does not Islam forbid representation of human figures? These were the questions that my French friend Jacques bombarded me with when I told him about feminine images in Muslim paintings.

The Muslim world has a fantastic tradition of painting, in which the Persian genius especially expressed itself fully. Romance was celebrated, as well as epic voyages and battles, and women were well represented. Often, they were depicted as aggressively involved in changing the world and constantly on the move—riding horses like Princess Shirin in "Khusraw and Shirin," or camels, like Zuleikha in the biblical story of Joseph. But, before going any further, let us address the question of Islam's censorship of human representation.

The censorship of images in Islam began mostly because the pagan Arabs worshiped no fewer than 360 idols in the temple of the Kaaba, the shrine of Mecca. According to the eighth-century author Hisham Ibn al-Kalbi, one of the few historians to describe the pagan pre-Islamic scene, some of these were *ançab*, or simple stones, and others were *açnam*, or statues of human figures.[1] The pre-Islamic Arabs also fabricated small clay statues of their favorite gods to protect their homes, in their practice of domestic cults. Many of these worshiped divinities were goddesses, which could be an additional reason for Islam's ban on representation. The Prophet's own tribes worshiped three Arab goddesses—Al-lat, al Uzza, and Manat.

When the Prophet conquered Mecca, he destroyed the pagan divinities, cleaned the shrine, and declared that only one God should be worshiped.[2] The exact verse of the Koran that bans images also forbids three other sins: wine, gambling, and divination. "O ye who believe! Strong drink (*khamr*) and games of chance (*maysir*) and idols (*ançab*) and divining arrows (*azlam*) are only an infamy of Satan's handiwork. Leave it aside in order that ye may succeed" (Sura 5:89).[3] However, we know that not all Muslims are angels; some drink wine, others gamble, yet others—mostly women—indulge in divination and magical practices, and some paint representational images. Certain nations, such as Persia, already had a strong artistic tradition when they came to Islam and did not stop producing representational images simply because of their new religion. On the contrary, the Persians enriched Muslim culture by introducing to it their impressive cultural heritage, and taught Arabs and others the art of miniature painting. Persian artists were often invited to the Turkish and Mughal courts to help produce illustrated manuscripts in book-making ateliers.

Two more reasons explain why the ban on representational images was not enforced throughout the Muslim world. The first is that Muslims made a logical distinction between religious art and secular art. Inside the mosque, unlike inside the church, there were—and are—no representational images. But in the homes of wealthy men, miniature paintings were prized, and some powerful caliphs and sultans even had their own artists' ateliers. Unlike in the West, the rich did not think about sharing their paintings with the poor, and even today, most Muslim art is still in the hands of the rich and the powerful. The concept of the museum is purely a Western import, which explains why museums in our part of the world are usually poorly endowed, ill equipped, and often deserted. The second reason that representational art has always existed in Muslim countries is that Islam has no sacred clergy, as does the Catholic Church, for example, to enforce conformity.

There is no such thing as an infallible religious authority such as the pope in orthodox Islam, for instance.

So, what kind of images of women do we find in Muslim painting? What happens to emotions and the power structure in cultures where men dare to transgress God's recommendation to avoid human representations and go ahead and paint their fantasies? How did these daring Muslim men represent women and the emotions such women stirred in them? Did these men respect the *Shari'a* (religious law), with its ideal of the harem and sexual segregation, or did they violate it? Bencheikh, one of the most eloquent of Arab writers, summarizes it thus, in words that apply as much to today's world as yesterday's: "Love opens horizons and destabilizes certainties. A man in love invents himself as something other than what he was. A woman in love discovers the multiple selves that one desires in her. Freedom in love is conceived of as surmounting and going beyond the limits of the self."[4]

To help us understand the ideal of feminine beauty in Muslim fantasies, as expressed in painting, let us focus on Princess Shirin, who was a purely secular heroine and is one of the most painted women in Muslim art. Like Scheherazade, Shirin is a Persian name. But if Scheherazade is a literary heroine, Shirin is her equivalent in art. A secluded princess who leaves the harem of her birth the moment she falls in love, she is often portrayed riding alone through the woods, chasing after Prince Khusraw, or bathing in isolated ponds, with her horse keeping a watchful eye over the scene. When she finally finds Prince Khusraw, the two of them are portrayed hunting wild beasts together, and when Khusraw "sabers a lion" to impress her, she instantly reciprocates by spearing a wild ass.[5] And if we are to judge by the miniature paintings of her adventures, Shirin is not disturbed one bit, as I would have been, by the death of the wild beasts. Her features are calm; her heart is not bleeding with tenderness.

I could not help but laugh out loud when I went back to the Louvre to compare my Muslim miniatures with Ingres's odalisques—they were so different. I tried to imagine what would have happened if Ingres had met Shirin face to face in the Bois de Boulogne woods. Would he have stripped her of her arrows and horse in order to paint her? Would he have taken away her silk caftan and clothes as well? And what about Immanuel Kant, who said knowledge kills a woman's charm, so that an educated woman might as well have a beard? At the thought of a fake beard under Shirin's lovely chin, I started laughing so merrily that the elegant French security guard on the Louvre's solemn and dark first floor, where *La Grande Odalisque* is imprisoned forever, asked me to either chuckle more quietly or leave at once. I chose the second option and headed toward the rue de Rivoli exit, with my head up.

The romance of "Khusraw and Shirin" is part of the *Khamseh* ("Quintet") written by the poet Nizami (1140–1209). It has been illustrated innumerable times by Muslim painters, be they Persian, Turk, or Mughal. Shirin and her beloved Khusraw came from different countries: Khusraw was a Persian prince, the son of King Hurmuzd, and Shirin was the niece of the Queen of Armenia. Though this is typical of Muslim legends and tales, as though preparing us for an unavoidable pluralism to come, one can't help but wonder how they came to know each other, especially since the princess was secluded in her aunt's luxurious palace. Well, Khusraw first fell in love with Shirin in a dream; he "dreamed he would ride the world's fastest horse, Shabdiz, and gain a sweet and beautiful wife named Shirin."[6] Soon thereafter, Khusraw heard from his friend Shapur, who had visited Armenia, about a lovely princess named Shirin, the niece of that country's queen. When Shapur realized how powerful his friend's passion for his dream woman was, he rode back to Armenia with a strategic plan that worked beautifully: "Shapur sparked Shirin's interest by hanging portraits of Khusraw on trees and explained how she could join the prince in Persia."[7] And guess what? The secluded princess did not hesitate a minute. Instead, she simply jumped on "the fastest horse in the world" and started her irresistible, impulsive journey in search of love. And, "after fourteen days and nights, exhausted and covered with dust, she came to a gentle pool and stopped to bathe."[8] What a singular moment, that extraordinary point in time when a secluded woman turns into an adventurer, rides alone for weeks through strange forests, and then stops to bathe in a wild river as if it was all completely natural. Shirin bathing in the wilderness has been obsessively celebrated by Muslim miniature painters ever since.

Meanwhile, Khusraw, forced by political events to leave Persia, was riding in the opposite direction, toward Armenia, when he happened upon a beauty bathing in a pool, her aristocratic identity betrayed by her magnificently adorned horse waiting nearby. This scene of "Khusraw watching Shirin bathing," wherein the heroine is depicted as a mysterious horsewoman swimming in wild forests, is another landmark of Muslim miniatures.[9] But, of course, during this first encounter, neither Shirin nor Khusraw spoke to each other—otherwise we would have no legend. Instead, "astounded by her beauty, Khusraw quietly drew closer. Startled, Shirin hid herself in her long tresses, dressed, and rode off. Although Khusraw desired the exquisite maiden for his own, he never guessed her identity. Nor did Shirin recognize Khusraw, though later she wondered if the handsome horseman was the prince."[10] Both lovers then departed, looking for each other in opposite directions, a theme universal in its pathos, because we all spend our brief lives doing just that, even if we physically share our beds with the same person every night for years. Always we carry an image in our head of a better partner, of an ideal person, which blurs our chances of finding happiness.

Falling in love with an image or picture is, I guess, an allegory of what happens to all of us. We start our emotional quest for happiness with an image tattooed on our childhood psyches, and cross days and nights, rivers and oceans, looking for that ideal someone who comes closest to our fantasy picture. The love motifs in Muslim painting and storytelling remind us that happiness is about traveling far to meet the different other. Falling in love is about crossing boundaries and taking risks.

Falling in love with an image is a theme echoed in many of the tales in *The Thousand and One Nights*. In "The Prince Who Fell in Love with the Picture," for example, a Persian prince is captivated by the portrait of a woman from Ceylon. This implies a lot of travel, as we can surmise from the following summary: "A young prince entered his father's treasury one day, and saw a little cedar chest set with pearls, diamonds, emeralds, and topazes. . . . On opening it (for the key was in the lock) he beheld the picture of an exceedingly beautiful woman, with whom he immediately fell in love. Ascertaining the name of the lady from an inscription on the back of the portrait, he set off with a companion to find her. Having been told by an old man at Baghdad that her father at one time reigned in Ceylon, he continued his journey thither, encountering many unheard of adventures along the way."[11]

Love between a man and a woman is by necessity a hazardous blending of alien cultures, if only because of the sexual difference, which is a cosmic frontier, an existential boundary. In the Muslim psyche, to love is to learn about crossing the line to meet the challenge of the difference. It is also about discovering the wonderful richness of humanness, the plurality, the diversity of Allah's creatures. One of the most quoted verses of the Koran, and one that I particularly love, reads: "And we made you into different nations and tribes, so that you may know about each other" (Sura 49:12). The Arabic word "to know" in this verse, *'arafa,* comes from *'Arif,* meaning a leader chosen by his group because he has accumulated knowledge by asking many questions about things he did not know.[12] To understand this Muslim emphasis on learning from differences, one has to remember that Islam originated in the desert (present-day Saudi Arabia) and that Mecca's prosperity as a center of trade in the first years of the Muslim calendar was due to travelers constantly crossing through on roads linking Africa with Asia and Europe. Unlike the racist stereotype that most Westerners have of Islam, which they reduce to a *jihad,* or sacred war, this religion spread from Arabia to Indonesia through trade routes, via travelers talking to one another and learning from one another's cultures. Writes historian Marshall Hodgson: "During the five centuries after 945 (Abbasid dynasty), the former society of the caliphate was replaced by an international society that was constantly expanding, linguistically and culturally, ruled by numerous independent governments. This society was not held together by a single political order or a single language or culture. Yet it did remain, consciously and effectively, a single historical whole. In its time, this international Islamicate society was certainly the most widely spread and influential society on the globe."[13] That fascinating and enriching diversity is a strong message that comes through in many Muslim fantasies, and I think it explains why citizens in my part of the world are so interested in the Internet and digital technology, despite widespread illiteracy and poverty.[14] (Although the unexpected mushrooming of "cyber-cafés" in Moroccan shantytowns may also be due to young people trying to connect with strangers and thereby obtain visas to emigrate![15])

In the early Muslim world, discovering other cultures meant fantasizing about the opposite sex. Sindbad never missed an opportunity to fall in love, and married whenever he reached a new island, taking advantage of his right to be polygamous. To take the risk of falling in love with a foreign woman, and vice versa, is a powerful dream in many Muslim legends, tales, and paintings. Sometimes, to dramatize the "foreignness" of a woman for a man in love, she is described as being an extraterrestrial creature. Such is the case in the tale of "Jullnar of the Sea," which Scheherazade narrates to Shahrayar on their two hundred and thirtieth night. Jullnar is discovered on the seashore by a slave trader, who sells her to the king who rules the land. The king falls madly in love with her, largely because she behaves quite strangely. Jullnar shares his bed and shows him tenderness when they make love, yet sometimes he catches her behaving in mysterious ways. It is the tiny things, the small gestures, that make men realize how great is the distance separating them from the women they embrace. In Jullnar's case, the sea often seems to attract her more than the king who loves and cherishes her: "When in the evening, the king went in to her, he saw her standing at the window, looking at the sea, but although she noticed his presence, she neither paid attention to him nor showed him veneration, but continued to look at the sea, without even turning her head toward him."[16] Yes, the feminine as the locus of strangeness and unpredictability haunts Islam, the only world religion that legally enforces women's seclusion through *Shari'a,* or sacred law.

Women in love in Muslim miniatures always have some sort of problem, which they often solve by taking boats and crossing oceans. Shirin has to do this as well, and as we see in many of the paintings depicting her sea voyage, her entire crew is female.[17] This comes as no surprise to a woman such as myself, reared in a traditional household, since my illiterate grandmother nurtured my imagination long ago by telling me about Ghalia, the Moroccan equivalent of Shirin. From age three to thirty, when television reached Morocco, and silenced the grandmothers, I heard the story of Ghalia again and again. Daily, Ghalia jumped "seven seas, seven rivers, and seven channels" to solve what at first seemed insoluble problems. And on the day I took off on a flight from

Casablanca to Malaysia for my first conference there in 1987, I remembered Ghalia and felt that my grandmother would have approved of me if she were still alive. The message that you got as a little girl in my Muslim world, before television, was that life is tough, and that in order to reach the imaginary palace of the legendary prince, you had better be ready to perform wonders like Ghalia because nothing is easy or certain. Older women would tell little girls, "You have to work hard to snatch a little minute of happiness." Yes, I was never told that life was going to be easy for me. Never. I was told that even a minute of happiness involves much work and concentration. I was never told that a prince would make me happy. Instead I was told that I could create happiness if I concentrated enough, and that I could make the prince happy—and vice versa—if I liked him enough.

Princes in Muslim tales and legends always have problems as well. Even if a woman is deeply loved and living in a luxurious harem, you can expect her prince to get into political trouble and his dynasty to come to an end. A woman must always be ready to jump onto a horse and cross alien territories: Uncertainty is a woman's destiny. And to finish Shirin's story, she keeps on riding and riding through unknown lands, encountering numerous unexpected adventures, until she finally meets and marries Khusraw. Her unlimited energy is an inspiration to Muslim painters and to Muslim women as well.

Mobility as an important characteristic of the beloved

woman is also central to Sufi mystics like Ibn 'Arabi, who describes the female lover as being *Tayyar,* or, literally, "endowed with wings"[18]—an idea that the Muslim miniature painters often tried to capture. When Ibn 'Arabi undertook his long journey to Mecca in the thirteenth century, he was forced to reflect on the nature of love, that extraordinary feeling that gives human beings a chance to reach toward divine perfection.[19] It is well known that the Sufi mystics, starting with Ibn 'Arabi, have always had trouble drawing a line between love inspired by the divine and love inspired by a woman.

Ibn 'Arabi was born in Muslim Spain, in Murcia, in 1155, and undertook the journey to Mecca, six thousand miles away, in search of spiritual teachers who would help him grow. But he fell in love—not part of his plan—when he was admitted to the home of his teacher, Imam Ibn Rustum. "When I sojourned in Mecca in 585 [1206 in the Christian calendar]," Ibn 'Arabi writes, "I met there a group of excellent persons, men and women, highly educated and virtuous. But the most virtuous of all . . . was the master and learned Imam Abu Shaja' Zahir Ibn Rustum. . . . This master, may God have mercy on him, had a daughter, a slender virgin, who charmed whoever looked at her, and whose presence enriched conferences and introduced happiness in the hearts of its speakers. Her name was Nizam." What seduced Ibn 'Arabi above all was Nizam's intelligence: "She was a religious sciences expert *(alima)* . . . She had magic eyes *(sahirat at-tarf)*, Iraqi wit *('iraqiatu ad-*

*darf*) . . ." And Nizam, as one might expect, was also eloquent: "When she decides to express herself, she makes her
message clear" (*in afçahat, awdahat*) and "when she decides
to be brief, she is incomparably concise" (*in awjazat,
a'jazat*).[20] Nizam's quick mind enabled her to captivate
everyone's attention in the *majliss,* or intellectual gather-
ings, that her father held in his house.

What is remarkable about Ibn 'Arabi's story is that he decided to make his erotic feelings for Nizam public, instead
of keeping them to himself, because for him the difference
between divine love and the erotic transport that an eloquent woman can stir in a man is slight. In one of his
poems, which was scandalous then, and is still regarded as a
sinful document by some today, Ibn 'Arabi tries to clarify
his emotional turmoil by describing how easy it is for the
boundaries between the divine and the erotic to vanish.
Conservative religious authorities in Aleppo, Syria, condemned Ibn 'Arabi's poem as nothing more than a prurient,
lust-filled document with no spiritual content whatsoever.
And that is when Ibn 'Arabi took up his pen to write *Translator of Desires* (*Turjuman al Ahswaq*), a fascinating book
about love as enigma and cosmic mystery. In it, he tries to
translate the subtleties of desire for the rigid conservatives
who were unable to grasp sophisticated feelings. But paradoxically, in so doing, Ibn 'Arabi confirms the slippery nature of attraction and the yearning of all human beings to
cross boundaries toward the "other," be it the opposite sex

or the divine. This celebration of sensuality as mobile energy, so strong in Sufism, also seems to animate Muslim artists when they portray adventurous women crossing rivers on fast horses, and vividly contradicts the morbid passivity of women that we find in Western harems.

A few days before I left Paris, Christiane, my French editor, invited me to one of her favorite restaurants, in order to share with me some of her insights into the Frenchmen's harem fantasy. She warned me in advance that "Le Restaurant du Louvre" was pretentious, *très bourgeois,* and not very welcoming to tourists—all of which I found to be true. As I entered the restaurant, I felt as if I were stepping into a very exclusive French household whose rituals I was likely to violate, just because I came from another culture. My heavy, noisy silver bracelets and necklace looked utterly *déplacé* and so did my jacket, which was nothing more than a colorful shortened caftan. But when Christiane came in, heads turned to look at her with appreciative admiration. Like most French women in important positions, she always dresses in black, and in unusually bold outfits. On that day, she was wearing a Yamamoto stretch silk dress with one shoulder totally bare, and looked down at the crowd as if she had just landed from a much more refined planet. "Remember what I told you about the pretentiousness of this restaurant," she murmured while seating herself on one of the luxurious gilded sofas. "This is one of the rare spots in Paris where aristocrats have the guts to exhibit their family jewelry to proletarians like me who have to work eight hours a day to pay taxes to the Republic."

I could not refrain from laughing. I am always amazed at how revolutionary the French are in their daily discourse, constantly attacking the privileged classes and the priests, all while voting to maintain both in office. Before calling for the waiter, Christiane took out her mirror and lipstick and started making herself up, as if we were entirely alone, while calmly continuing to study the "aristocrats."

"Can you believe it?" she said. "Two centuries after the Revolution, the aristocrats are just as insolent as ever." Christiane's voice could definitely be heard by our neighbors, but she didn't seem to care. Instead, she focused on her mirror and ran her hand through her short blond hair, making it look even wilder than it already did.

I admire French women because they don't hesitate to get into fights in cafés, demanding that waiters not neglect them, while I hesitate to squander my energies fighting in Moroccan public places, where men often push women aside to get to the head of queues. Vicariously, I enjoy witnessing my Parisian friends' ceaseless revolution. However, this time, I wanted Christiane to stop her republican crusade and focus on a more urgent matter.

"Is there a link between Kant's philosophical concept of beauty and Ingres's passive model of the harem beauty?" I asked her. "Someone has to clear this up for me so that I can give my poor mind a rest for a while."

Christiane started by reminding me that in the West, men had kept women out of the arts professions for centuries, and forbade them, just as the Greeks had their slaves long before them, from painting pictures. She quoted Margaret Miles, an American professor of the history of theology, who stated that "The social practice of professional painting also insisted on the painter's maleness, as academies in which figure drawing and painting from nude models were taught did not admit women until the end of the eighteenth century."[21] Christiane was surprised that I hardly knew anything about a new branch of art literature that focuses on *"Le Regard"* ("The Gaze"), and started dictating all the titles that she thought I ought to read on that topic—when I interrupted her. "Don't give me any more books to read—just summarize the essentials," I begged her, not wanting to have to pay any more excess-luggage duties than I already undoubtedly faced, when taking the Paris-Casablanca flight. Christiane complied by saying that for centuries in her culture, painting, just like thinking, was considered to be an exclusively male privilege. "And what do I mean by the gaze?" Christiane contemplated, sipping her glass of champagne. "Well, look, Western men did not, for example, unlike the painters of Muslim miniatures, represent themselves in the harems they painted. In Ingres's harem, you don't find the male partner. Maybe a slave occasionally, but not the master."

I felt startled—she was right. I had been stupid not to notice that before.

"Eroticism in Western painting," Christiane went on, "was always a male observer looking at a nude woman he paralyzes in a frame."

Christiane then stated that, like I, she was absolutely convinced there was a logical connection between philosophy and art, between Kant and Ingres. "Even now," she said, "I still hear the unavoidable *'Soie belle et tais-toi'*—be beautiful and shut up—both in the workplace and in personal relations. . . . Fatema, you have to remember that the play *Les Femmes Savantes,* in which Molière makes fun of women who aspire to be educated, was still being taught while I was in public school, and we are talking about the 1960s." To prove her point, Christiane recited by heart the passage from the play wherein Clitandre, one of Molière's male characters, stresses how much he dislikes educated women:

Intellectual women are not to my taste. I grant you, a woman should know all sorts of things. But I cannot abide a woman who feels the deplorable urge to learn simply to become learned. When such matters crop up in conversation, I'd rather she knew enough not to know what she knows.[22]

The seventeenth century, Christiane went on—that century of enlightenment, when humanism and the cult of reason flourished—was also the century of Molière and other like-minded men, who achieved enormous success by belittling educated women. "Molière wrote his *Femmes Savantes* in 1672," Christiane said, "but even before then, he had made the whole French court laugh at educated women in plays such as *Les Précieuses ridicules* (1659) and *École des femmes* (1663). In all of them, women who aspired to educate themselves about scientific discoveries were portrayed as ugly and repulsive." No wonder, she concluded, that there were men like Jacques who dreamt of harems filled with passive odalisques and trembled with fear whenever they were attracted to a professional woman.

I kept silent when Christiane started talking about Jacques—I certainly was not going to tell her that he was hoping to kidnap her to a deserted island. She then told me that she had bought a book for his birthday—*Ways of Seeing* by John Berger. Could you please summarize the main message of that book for me? I pleaded again—what is it exactly that you want Jacques to understand? Nodding, Christiane said that Berger condenses the whole Western history of visual images of women into one five-word sentence: "Men act and women appear." Elaborating, she then quoted another key Berger phrase: "Men look at women. Women watch themselves being looked at."[23] So it's no wonder, Christiane concluded, that "image" is a major weapon used by Western men to dominate women.

But how does all this work in Paris, I asked her, where

women have invaded the professions and compete with men in all kinds of jobs?

"Yes, sure, women get the jobs," Christiane said. "But everywhere you see powerful men surrounding themselves with younger women to destabilize the older and more mature women who have reached higher positions. A French company might be housed in a modern glass building on the Champs Elysées, but inside, the atmosphere is still that of a repressive harem. Men feel insecure or jealous when women in senior positions insist on earning as much as they do."

As we were about to leave the restaurant, Christiane had an interesting flash of insight regarding the Orient. "I wondered when I read your pages about women in Muslim miniatures," she said, "if the fact that the artists were often attached to the caliph's or king's palace did not give the harem women a certain amount of power over what was painted."

Immediately, the name of Nur-Jahan came to my mind. The wife of the Mughal emperor Jahangir, Nur-Jahan managed, despite her harem seclusion, to influence not only politics but also art. In sixteenth-century India, she dictated to artists how to portray women, and commissioned some of the best ones, living in the imperial court's ateliers, to paint her armed with a rifle.

"If this Nur-Jahan is not a figment of your imagination, but a historical person who really existed," Christiane said, "she might provide us with a clue as to why Western women did not influence painting."

I pricked up my ears. "Be more explicit," I begged.

"Unlike harem women like Nur-Jahan, who, as the wife of the emperor, was the buyer of the painting, in the West, it was typically men who bought paintings."

How interesting, I thought. It really does pay to provoke foreigners to solve your mysteries for you.

---

1. Hisham Ibn al-Kalbi, *Kitab al Açnam* (Paris: Librairie Klincksieck, 1969), p. 16. This Arabic edition comes with an excellent French translation by Wahid Atallah.

2. For more on the political background on the ban on images, see Chapter Six of my book *Islam and Democracy* (New York: Addison Wesley, 1992), p. 85 and following.

3. Translated by Mohammed Marmaduke Pickthall as Sura 5:90 in *The Meaning of the Glorious Koran* (New York: Mentor Books, n.d.), p. 104.

4. From: "L'exigence d'Aimer," interview of Jamal Bencheikh by Fethi Benslama and Thierry Fabre in *Qantara* magazine, N° 18, Jan., Feb., Mar. 1996. (*Qantara* is the magazine of the Paris-based Institut du Monde Arabe.)

5. Commentary on the painting by B. W. Robinson, "Persian Paintings in the Indian Office Library: A descriptive catalogue" (London: Sotheby Parke Bernet, 1976), p. 25. A color reproduction showing Shirin armed with arrows exists in the same book in the color plate section: Colour plate N° III. N° 138: *"Khusraw and Shirin in the hunting-field—Tabriz style, 1530."*

6. Stuart Cary Welch, *Wonders of the Age: Masterpieces of Early Safavid Painting, 1501–1576* (Boston: Fogg Art Museum, Harvard University, 1979), p. 150.

7. Ibid.

8. Ibid.

9. The most ravishing rendering of this scene is the one in the British Library, from the "Khusray and Shirin" executed during Shah Tahmasp's Quinted of Nizami portfolio, ascribed to the painter Sultan Muhammad. See reproduction in Welch's *Wonders of the Age: Masterpieces of Early Safavid Painting*, ibid., p. 150.

10. Ibid.

11. Richard F. Burton, Supplemental Nights to "The Book of the 1001 Nights

and a Night" (London: Burton Club for Private Subscribers, 1886), op. cit., vol. II, p. 328.

12. See the word *'arafa* in *Lissan al 'Arab* ("The Tongue of the Arabs"), a thirteenth-century dictionary by Ibn Manzhur (Cairo: Dar al Maarif, 1979).

13. Marshall Hodgson, *The Venture of Islam*, vol. II, "The Expansion of Islam in the Middle Period" (Chicago: The University of Chicago Press, 1974).

14. See the special issue on "Digital Islam" by SIM newsletter N° 2 of March 1999. SIM is published by the International Institute of Study of Islam in the Modern World, Leiden, the Netherlands (http:isim.leidenuvin.nl).

15. See Mohammed Zainabi, "La démocratisation de l'Internet: coup d'oeil sur les cybers au Maroc," in the Moroccan daily *L'opinion*, August 12, 1999. It is very likely that the Internet will encourage illiterate citizens to teach themselves to read instead of waiting for their bureaucratic governments' ridiculously inefficient "literacy programs." The accessibility of training on the Internet makes this possible, as Youssef Moumile so rightly explains in his article, "Quelle stratége gouvernementale pour internet," p. 32 of *Le Journal*, one of Morocco's avant-garde weeklies (e.mail: media@macronet.net.ma).

16. Haddawy, *Arabian Nights*, op. cit., p. 386.

17. One example is the "Sea-Voyage of Shirin," Qazwin style, 1580, in "Persian Paintings" by Robinson, op. cit., p. 61.

18. "C'est un trait de l'amant que la mobilité" Ibn 'Arabi "Traité de L'amour," translated by Maurice Gloton, Albin Michel, 1986. Page 205. This short essay on love selected by the French translator is part of Ibn 'Arabi's multi-volume masterwork *"Al Futuhat al Makkiya" (The Book of spritual Mekka Conquests)*.

19. It was in Mecca in 1203 that Ibn 'Arabi started writing his multi-volume masterwork *Al Futuhat al Makkiya (The Book of Spiritual Mekka Conquests)*.

20. My translation from the Arabic original of *Turjuman al Ashwaq* (Beirut: Dar Çader, 1966), p. 11.

21. Margaret Miles, *Carnal Knowing: Female Nakedness and Religious Meaning in the Christian West* (New York: Vintage Books, 1991), p. 14.

22. Translated to English by John Wood and David Coward in Molière's *The Misanthrope And Other Plays* (London: Penguin Books, 1959), p. 264.

23. John Berger, *Ways of Seeing* (New York: Penguin, 1977), p. 47.

# 12

# Princess Nur-Jahan Chases Tigers

Nur-Jahan (Light of the World) was born Nur-Mahal (Light of the Palace), but the first thing she did after marrying Emperor Jahangir in 1611 was to change her name. She also wanted everyone to know that her favorite pastime was hunting tigers, of which she killed many, competing with the best in the field: "During her time on the throne, Nur-Jahan gained a reputation as a superb markswoman, surpassing even Mirza Rustam, Jahangir's best shot, in the killing of tigers."[1] In this context, it is interesting to recall that Ingres's favorite pastime was playing the violin. An early portrait of him at age thirty-eight, painted in Rome in 1818 by J. Alaux, depicts the artist playing the violin in his studio, while his new wife Madeleine, standing outside, looks on with admiration. It would be difficult to find the equivalent of J. Alaux's portrait in Muslim miniatures. A Muslim artist would probably depict the woman playing the musical instrument (or hunting wild animals) while the man looked on. But Nur-Jahan's most spectacular coup was not the shooting of tigers but the influencing of artists.

A stunning—and revolutionary—Mughal miniature, *Jahangir and Prince Khurram Feasted by Nur-Jahan*, dated 1617, hangs in the Freer Gallery of Art in Washington, D.C. (Smithsonian Institution). The painting is a turning point in the history of Islamic painting in general and the depiction of harem women in particular for at least three reasons. The first is that the artist painted an accurate likeness of Emperor Jahangir and Queen Nur-Jahan. Up until then, most Islamic miniatures, painted predominantly by Persian artists, reproduced legendary figures, such as mythical kings from the *Shah-nameh*, Persia's national epic; Princess Shirin of the *Khamsaeh*, the romance poem written by Nizami; or biblical figures such as King Solomon and the Queen of Sheba. The Mughal, in contrast, were the first to introduce to miniatures the portrait in the Western sense of the word—that is, to precisely reproduce the features of the sovereign in order to boost the "present ruler's legitimacy."[2] In a word, the Mughal were the first Muslims to introduce the painted image as an instrument of political propaganda—just like the Renaissance French or British kings—something previously unheard of in any Islamic court.[3]

The miniature of Jahangir, Prince Khurram, and Nur-

Jahan is also revolutionary in that the artist did not paint the Emperor alone, but rather, sitting with his wife. This meant that this Muslim queen, who was supposed to be secluded and hidden in a harem, was unveiled. When you remember that even today, many Muslim heads of state, such as the King of Saudi Arabia, still seclude their wives, who are rarely seen during official receptions, you realize just how subversive Nur-Jahan was.

The third reason this miniature painting marks a turning point in Islamic art is that the queen is portrayed as the host: "Although Jahangir is still the dominant figure . . . he now shares the viewer's attention with Nur-Jahan, who is not only clearly in charge but supported as well by an army of women."[4] So, not only had the queen taken the lead, she had also commissioned the court's artists to celebrate *her* event: the ceremony she organized in Mandu in October 1617 to honor Prince Khurram, Jahangir's son by another woman, after his conquest of the Indian province of the Deccan. This ceremony was eminently political, attracting numerous ambassadors of foreign powers, including Sir Thomas Roe of England.[5] Also, last but not least, the miniature's tiny details, such as "the cups of wine, the luxurious textures of cloth and stone, and the open necklines and midriffs," indicate that something new was happening in the lives of harem women—thanks to one woman's initiative, they were no longer quite so invisible as they had been.

The basis of misogyny in Islam is actually quite weak, resting only on the distribution of space. If women invade public space, male supremacy is seriously jeopardized. And in actuality, modern Muslim men have already lost their power base, as their monopoly over public space has been eroded with the massive entrance of women into scientific fields and the professions.[6] My esteemed Islamist colleague at Mohamed V University, Professor Benkiki, produced these UNESCO statistics one day when I stepped into the staff room: "If Islamic politicians are still allergic to women in parliaments," he cried, exhibiting the UNESCO document, "women have organized their silent revenge by invading the worlds of sciences and technical professions in huge numbers. Today, 28.7% of the scientific and technical positions in Egypt are filled by women, 29.3% in Turkey, 27.6% in Algeria, and 31.3% in Morocco."[7] Trust a conservative man, I thought as he spoke, to correctly analyze women's situation. In oil-fueled fundamentalist regimes, women's appetite for scientific fields is even stronger: One third of all the scientists and technicians in the Islamic Republic of Iran are veiled ladies (32.6%). Kuwait's oil-drenched sheiks still deny women the right to vote, but 36% of the country's scientific "manpower" is female. Indonesian and Malaysian women also seem insatiable, holding down 40% and 44.5% of their respective countries' scientific positions.

Only when we keep in mind Islam's long tradition of

strong-minded women such as Nur-Jahan does the widespread emergence of professional women in modern Islamic societies make any sense—a precedent for them was
set long ago. This precedent also helps to explain why, in
Iran, Imam Khomeini's decision to force women to veil
only politicized Iranian women and made them bolder.
"Young women," explains writer Haleh Esfandiari, "found
ways to conform and yet challenge Islamic dress—showing
a puff of hair, called *Kakol,* under their scarves, using lipstick and nail polish despite the 'morals police.' In myriad
ways, they have reclaimed the public space."[8] Esfandiari's
book, based on interviews with dozens of women reflecting on the changes the Islamic Revolution brought to their
lives, shows that forcing women to veil can be a drastic incentive for an ambitious woman to rebel. Which brings us
back to Nur-Jahan. How did she conduct her revolution
from the harem?

How did Nur-Jahan present herself to the crowds? Did
she have a strategy for visibility? It seems that she did: One
of the images she often projected of herself was that of a bejeweled silk-clad warrior. In 1612, one year after her marriage, the best artist of India, Abu al-Hasan, painted *Portrait
of a Lady with a Rifle,* and many scholars believe that this
"may best tell us what she looked like. The untouched nat-
uralism of her face, the strength of character so loved by
portrait painters, the outdoor venue away from ordinary
seclusion, and the signature of Abu al-Hasan the King's fore-

most painter of the time who is more likely than any other to have been allowed into her presence, all argue for this as the most authentic image we now have"[9] of the Mughal queen." But this also begs the question: Was Nur-Jahan the exception, the only woman who enjoyed hunting in Mughal India, or was hunting a common female pastime?

Originally, the Mughal were rugged nomads, Turkified Mongols from Central Asia who traced their ancestry back to Genghis Khan, worshiped nature, and tried to re-create the wild outdoors in the gardens that they planted at their palaces. They also had a tradition of outdoor sports, played by both men and women; "Women had been using bows and arrows and playing polo for decades and, from accounts of early Mughal harems, women bearing arms guarded the protective Zanana enclosures."[10] *Zanana* is the Hindu equivalent of "odalisque."[11]

The spectacular visibility of women in outdoor ceremonies among the Muslim Turks and Mongols from Central Asia has always baffled Arab travelers, who reveal themselves, in their descriptions of this phenomenon, to be the most conservative of all Muslims on the seclusion and veiling of women. In 1334, the Moroccan traveler Ibn Batouta—the Muslim equivalent of Marco Polo—crossed Central Asia on his way to China, and was amazed by the high level of respect to women paid by the Turks. "I witnessed in these lands something remarkable," he writes. "The high consideration accorded by the Turks to their women. Women enjoy among the Turks a higher position than men."[12] As a good Moroccan, Ibn Batouta was especially astonished when he saw a prince salute a woman. "The first time I saw the princess, she was riding in a chariot adorned with a sumptuous blue drape . . . many chariots filled with women at her service followed hers. . . . When she arrived in front of the Prince's house, she stepped out of her chariot and so did thirty women of her company. . . . She walked with majesty towards the Prince. . . . The prince stood up and walked towards her, saluted her, and invited her to take a seat besides his own. . . ."[13] Ibn Batouta also repeats many times, in his 750-page *Rihla* (Voyage), dictated in 1355, that "the women of the Turks do not veil . . . and you would often mistake the husband for the servant."[14] All of these comments help us to negate the stereotype, so common today, that Islam is 100% misogynous. Ibn Batouta's remarks show that there was and is no such thing as a unified Muslim culture. If Arabs veiled women and kept them in marginal positions, Turks and Mongols did not. This also helps us to better understand both sixteenth-century Mughal miniatures of women and how Nur-Jahan could have carved out such a prominent position for herself.

One of Nur-Jahan's assets was her age. She was not a young and blushing virgin when she married Jahangir in 1611, but a thirty-four-year-old widow whose husband, a dignitary who had held a post in Bengal, had died under mysterious circumstances. His death was suspicious because everyone knew that Jahangir had loved Nur-Jahan since childhood; "After the unexplained death of this embarrassing husband, she returned to the heart of the imperial court, and married Jahangir a few months later."[15] Another unusual detail was that Nur-Jahan was a foreigner in India—she was a Persian and, as such, a Shi'ite.[16] To marry Jahangir, who, like most Mughal rulers, belonged to a Sunni (orthodox) dynasty, was like sliding into a minefield. Yet Nur-Jahan was clever enough to create a Shi'a lobby within the court, by placing men of her family in key positions. She "surrounded herself with a clan comprising, among others, her father, Itimad ud-Dawla, a Persian adventurer who had become Jahangir's prime minister, and her brother Asaf Khan."[17]

But if Nur-Jahan had been merely a sportswoman or an astute harem lady who surrounded herself with men of her camp, she would not have had the extraordinary impact that she has had on the Islamic cultural scene in general and on the arts in particular. She also had a flair for public relations, on two distinct levels. First, she stepped directly into the artists' studios and negotiated new ways of representing women, love, and conjugal intimacy in art, by appearing beside her imperial husband at events she initiated. Second, she became involved as an art collector, thus indirectly influencing fashion and taste. "We know that Mughal women of the noble class and imperial family were considerable traders . . . running their own boats and developing their own list of commodities, and that of them, the two most illustrated were Jahangir's mother, Maryam al-Zaman, and Nur-Jahan. . . ."[18] Nur-Jahan's influence as an aggressive trader was so well known in diplomatic circles that between 1617 and 1618, she was even appointed "protectress" of the British Embassy.[19]

As Nur-Jahan was familiar with both Islamic and Western painting, she must have realized that her Mughal husband, Jahangir, who was half Indian, was not faithfully reproducing the tradition of the Persian miniature. She must have realized that he was using painting for political propaganda purposes by borrowing *darshana* from his Hindu childhood, and thereby framing himself as an Indian god.[20]

*Darshana,* which literally means "seeing" or "viewing," refers to the religious ritual of the Hindu gods, who occasionally reveal themselves to their worshipers, thus allowing them the privilege of gazing at their images. "Just as a Hindu god is said to give *darshana* to worshippers who gaze at its image," states Michael Brand, an expert in Indian art, so Mughal emperors "would appear for the public each morning at a special palace window and later to assembled nobles within the palace audience hall."[21]

In the Hindu tradition, a human being who is privileged enough to experience *darshana,* to gaze at the god he worships, is believed to catch some of his power. By "sighting a revered person, sacred image or place, and taking into oneself their inherent religious power, devotees of Hindu gods receive through the eye contact some of their magic energy."[22] But by elaborating on this Hindu *darshana*, the Mughal emperor broke a major taboo of original Islam: the prohibition of the personality cult. A Muslim ruler's primary qualification is modesty and humility. Al-Hakim, a Muslim ruler who pretended to be God in eleventh-century Egypt, for example, was immediately judged by the general Cairo population to be a crazy man who had lost his mind.[23] So it is only within this Hindu-influenced context that we can accurately understand the importance of the new Mughal miniature portraits with their accurate renderings of the Emperor's and Nur-Jahan's features.

Before leaving Nur-Jahan behind in the seventeenth century, I was tempted to ask the following question: Did Muslim history remember this incredibly subversive queen? To answer this query by myself would have taken hours or even days at the noisy and stuffy Rabat Mohamed V University library. But an Arab woman has at least one advantage over a man: If she calls an Islamic expert in fields such as history or *Shari'a* (religious law), and asks him for help, tradition decrees that he provide her with the requested information. The *Shari'a* expert that I usually contact often shows me the relevant pages in his own books and even lets me borrow them for a few days so that I can copy them. So I made a few telephone calls and within a few days was told about Omar Kahhala's portrayal of Nur-Jahan.

As recently as 1955, I learned, Omar Kahhala, an Egyptian scholar of Turkish origin, gave to Muslim women a fantastic gift: five volumes containing hundreds of profiles of "Women Celebrities in the Arab and Muslim World." Nur-Jahan, of course, is on the list, and Omar's description of her, which barely mentions her emperor husband, makes Scheherazade's princesses look miserably limited. "She was an Indian Queen, had grace and beauty," he writes. "She knew both Persian and Arabic and had a perfect knowledge of both cultures. She was accomplished in music and other sophisticated arts (*al adab ar-rafi'a*). She managed her kingdom in a perfectly rational manner, set taxes, and examined closely the country's daily affairs. She used to appear at a window of the palace to display herself to the kingdom's princes and to review armies' parades. Money was coined in her name which appeared together with that of her husband. It was reported that she used to go hunting with other women of her palace and that they rode the fastest of horses just like men."[24]

The passive odalisques painted by Ingres and his more modern heirs such as Matisse did not exist in the Orient! Persian miniatures held no secret for Matisse, who insisted on the importance of his 1910 visit to an Islamic art exhibition: "Persian miniatures . . . showed me the full possibility of my sensations."[25] And why wasn't Matisse interested in Kemal Ataturk's ideal of beauty, in Turkish women throwing away their veils and flying planes? It seems strange that in the 1920s an Oriental military man like Ataturk was dreaming of liberated women, while a man like Matisse, bred in a democracy, was dreaming of odalisques and an Islamic civilization that he confused with women's passivity.

What is the mystery behind the ideals of beauty inscribed in the psyches of men of different cultures? I kept asking my male university colleagues after I returned from my book tour, until Professor Benkiki, my favorite fundamentalist, silenced me with this remark:

"Fatema, why are you so obsessively preoccupied with what men think? A good Muslim woman your age should stop focusing on men and start doing something for illiterate women who need help from privileged women like you. Why don't you forget about men and focus on prayers so that Allah may forgive you your sins."

It took this extremely aggressive remark by my conservative colleague to alert me to the idea that my obsession was a good one. "If your idea disturbs a conservative man, hang on to it," I said to myself. "It will probably lead to important discoveries." Therefore, I stopped bombarding Professor Benkiki with questions concerning men's fantasies and accepted the fact that I would have to live with this enigma for months to come.

That next summer, I went to Temara Beach, between Rabat and Casablanca on the Atlantic Coast, and tried to forget about Ingres and Matisse and their harems. Instead, I listened to the roaring ocean, looked at the wonderful sunsets, and dove into the high tidal waves for hours when the moon was full. I did everything I could to forget about men's fantasies and thus conform to Professor Benkiki's definition of an ideal Muslim woman. I prayed and meditated, though I did so while standing in the ocean. This is a small but essential detail whose meaning probably escapes my dear colleague: Modern Muslim women have gained access to the ocean. They have pulverized the harem frontier and gained access to public spaces. Veiled or unveiled, we women are in the streets today by the millions. To meditate in a harem, sitting inside four walls, is completely different from meditating while standing in the Atlantic waves. In the ocean, I feel connected to the cosmos—I am as powerful as Scheherazade's "Lady with the Feather Dress." With access to state-paid education, computers, and the Internet, Muslim women have gained wings.

Kemal completely agrees with my theory that the ruling male elites of the Muslim world have already lost their battle against women, and that the extreme cases of violence against women that occur in Afghanistan and Algeria are a sign of the beginning of the end of misogynous Muslim despotism. "Women have emerged as a huge civic force pushing for democracy and fighting against injustice in our part of the world," he often says, "because basically, unlike in the Christian West, Muslim men believe women to be their equals. They grant them brains and energy and the capacity to rebel and challenge hierarchies. Now, Fatema, you are the winners."

When Kemal starts being so nice and supportive of me and of my theories, I start wondering if he is not just trying to seduce me again into making my aphrodisiac fish *tagine,* which involves a huge investment of time and money on my part. The most difficult thing is to find the supposedly aphrodisiac fish, the *Qurb,* in the first place. *Qurb* is the Arabic word for "coming closer," and ever since I first arrived in Rabat as a student, I have heard about its wonders. In my hometown of Fez, which is three hundred kilometers from the sea, we never knew that such a magical fish existed. But here, you can't get *Qurb* easily because the whole Rabat population is always looking for it, scavenging the fish markets along the beaches that stretch toward Casablanca. To increase your chances of finding the treasure, you have to be out searching at five A.M. But fortunately, at least we Rbati, or people from Rabat, don't have to compete with the three million citizens of Casablanca. The Casablanca people are like Americans: They focus on money, not sensuality.

Anyway, over the years I have learned so much about *Qurb,* and how to combine the right spices to make it a paradisiacal delight, that I have gained a reputation at the University, which has helped a lot in furthering my career. All of my male and female colleagues happily volunteer to provide me with any information I need in exchange for a bite of *Qurb.* And, of course, I keep my recipe a secret to protect my monopoly. Oh, I could tell you the ingredients that I use—a generous mix of fresh coriander, fresh ginger, garlic, and young olive oil from Chawen, a mountainous city near Tangier. But I am not going to divulge the proportions I use. . . .

So, you are beginning to understand what I mean by investing time and money in this precious *Qurb* tagine. Not that I am complaining, because the results are wonderful. However, it is not so much how you prepare the fish as the conditions under which you serve it that heighten its sensuality. The *Qurb* ought to be served on a terrace overlooking the ocean on the fourteenth night of a lunar month, when the moon is full and round. Yet even though I involved myself in various complicated but rewarding aphrodisiac recipes and spent many days swimming or just resting on the beach, my obsession with the European harem enigma kept taking hold of me.

As usual, whenever I am besieged by complicated questions I cannot answer, I behave as my grandmother Yasmina advised. "Forget about the whole thing," she often said. "Don't ever complicate your life. A woman's life is a tricky enough path as it is. Try to be good to yourself: Simplify things as much as you can." And that is when I decided not to finish this book. I stopped writing and started going to Mbarek, my favorite silver merchant's shop in the medina, to buy beads and try to focus on making some amber necklaces. I also tried, despite the rowdy Rabat traffic, to catch the sunsets at Temara Beach. Yes, indeed, I tried everything I could to avoid any kind of philosophical reflection on love, sex, and fear, and focused on the spectacular Atlantic sunsets instead. So intent was I on creating some sort of peace for myself that I talked no more about men's fantasies and harems.

A few years passed, and then one day, I woke up in a foreign city and realized, as so often happens when you are far from home, that I did not have the right clothes. I was in New York, it was summer, and my clothes felt uncomfortable. So I ran to buy a skirt in an American department store. And there, a small incident occurred that, just as in the Sufi tales, gave me a flash of enlightenment. Some of my questions about the Western harem enigma were finally answered.

---

1. Ellison Banks Findly, "Pleasure of Women: Nur Jahan and Mughal Painting" in "Patronage by Women in Islamic Art," *Asian Art,* Vol. 2, Spring 1993. Published by Oxford University Press in association with Arthur M. Sackler Gallery, Smithsonian Institution, p. 79.

2. Michael Brand, *The Vision of Kings: Art and Experience in India* (Canberra, Australia: National Gallery of Australia, 1995), p. 105.

3. "The most dramatic change in the depiction of Indian Kings occurred at the Mughal court of North India at the end of the sixteenth century. This change marked the first appearance of painted portraits in which the creation of an accurate likeness was of prime importance. Although earlier portraits often incorporated some individual traits, the aim had been to represent the power of the king rather than his personality. . . . This new portraiture (usually small in scale and bound into imperial manuscripts or albums) was made for a restricted court audience, as part of an attempt to forge a new imperial image based upon Indian, Islamic and European visual models. Within the palace libraries, these historical portraits were juxtaposed with images of mythical and divine rulers, boosting the present ruler's legitimacy." Brand, op. cit., p. 105.

4. Findly, op. cit., p. 78.

5. For Sir Thomas Roe's account of the Mughal Court, see *The Embassy of Sir Thomas Roe to the Court of the Great Mogul, 1615–1619, as Narrated in his Journal and Correspondence,* ed. William Foster (London: Hakluyt Society, 1899), vol. 2, p. 478.

6. This explains why so many conservative politicians and fundamentalist groups today, most linked to oil lobbies and interested in paralyzing democratic processes, invest money in promoting the veil, while statistics show that Muslim women have invaded many public spaces, including the labor market and the universities. See two of my recent articles that elucidate this link: F. Mernissi: "Palace Fundamentalism and Liberal Democracy: Oil, Arms and Irrationality" in "Social Futures, Global Visions," Special issue of *Development and Social Change,* Vol. 27, April 1996, pp. 251–265; and "Arab Women's Rights and the Muslim State in the Twenty-First Century: Reflections on Islam as Religion and State," in *Faith and Freedom: Women's Human Rights in the Muslim World* (Syracuse, N.Y.: Syracuse University Press, 1995), pp. 34–50.

7. The French version of UNESCO's 1997 "Human Development Report," which is where I got these statistics, uses the category of "Nombre de femmes dans l'encadrement et Fonctions techniques" (Chart 3, p. 172), which is defined thus on page 256: "Encadrement et Fonctions techniques: sont compris dans cette catégories les spécialistes le personnel technicien des domaines suivants: sciences physiques, architecture, ingénierie, aviation et marine (officiers inclus), sciences biologiques médecine, dentisterie, médecine vétérinaire, mathématiques, informatique, économie, comptabilité, droit, enseignement, religion, littérature, journalisme, sculpture, etc. . . . ."

8. Haleh Esfandiari, *Reconstructed Lives: Women and Iran's Islamic Revolution* (Washington, D.C.: The Woodrow Wilson Center Press, 1997), p. 6. See also Azar Nafissi, "Veiled Threat: The Iranian Revolution's Woman Problem," in *The New Republic,* February 22, 1999, and a more recent book by an American writer, Christian Bird "Neither East Nor West" (New York: Pocket Books, 2000).

9. Findly, op. cit., pp. 79–80.

10. Findly, op. cit., p. 79.

11. Hindus practiced *parda,* or the seclusion of women, just like their Muslim conquerors.

12. Ibn Batouta, *Rihla* (Voyage), written in 1355. The Arabic edition I use is that of Dar Beyrouth, 1985 edition, p. 329. An English edition with a commentary by H. Gibb was published in 1985, but I prefer to use my own translation. For a French edition, see the translation by de Defremery et Sanguinetti (1853–1859),

*Ibn Battûta: Voyage,* published in three volumes, La Découverte, Maspéro, 1982. Vol. II, p. 214.

13. Ibn Batouta, ibid., p. 330.

14. Ibid, p. 329.

15. Valerie Berinstain, *India and the Mughal Dynasty* (New York: Harry Abrams, 1997), p. 78.

16. The split of Islam into Sunni (orthodox) and Shi'a, which was at the beginning a split between Arabs with divergent interests, later became an instrument of Arab-Persian rivalry and Persian nationalism, known in Arabic as *shu'ubiya.* But it is only in the sixteenth century, under the Safavid dynasty, that Shi'ism became the official religion of Persia, now known as Iran. See Michel Mazzaoui, *The Origins of Safawids: Si'ism, Sufism, and the Gulat* (Weisbaden, Germany: Franz Steiner Verlag GMBH, 1972). On *shu'ubiya,* the Arab-Persian rivalry, from the Arab point of view, see the texts by Jahiz and others in Bernard Lewis, *Religion and Society* (New York: Harper and Row, 1974), chapter 9, "Ethnic Groups," page 199 and following. The Arab-Persian rivalry is manifested at the level of the language as well: Most of the people conquered by the Arabs forgot their previous language, history, and identity, and were merged into Arabic-speaking Islam. The Persians, however, sustained both by their recent memories of imperial greatness and by current awareness of their immense contribution to Islamic civilization, recovered and reasserted their separate identity. See Bernard Lewis, *Islam,* op. cit., vol. II, introduction. On the question of orthodoxy and dissent, see a short summary in "Orthodoxy and Shism" in H. Gibb, *Mohamedanism* (Oxford Univ. Press, 1980 reprint) p. 73 and following. A more in-depth analysis is that of Henri Corbin's section on "Le Chi'isme et la philosophie prophétique" (pp. 49–153) and on "La pensée Shi'ite" (pp. 437–496) in Henri Corbin, *Histoire de la Philosophie Islamique,* Gallimard, Paris, 1964.

17. Berinstain, op. cit., p. 78.

18. Findly, op. cit., p. 72.

19. Sir Thomas Roe, op. cit., 2:321. Also quoted in Findly, op. cit., p. 72.

20. One of the reasons for the longevity of the Mughal dynasty, which ruled India from 1526, when Muhamed Babur conquered Delhi, until the late 1800s, when Queen Victoria's British troops arrived, was their tolerance of the Hindu tradition, and their systematic borrowing from it. Previous to the Mughals, the Muslims had been trying to conquer India since the eighth century, but with little success.

21. Brand, op. cit., p. 106.

22. Brand, op. cit., p. 156.

23. For a brief sketch of al-Hakim, the ruler who pretended to be God, see my "Lady of Cairo" in F. Mernissi, *Forgotten Queens of Islam* (Minneapolis: University of Minnesota Press, 1993), pp. 179–189.

24. "Nur Jahan" in Omar Kahhala, *A'laam An Nissa* (Women's Who's Who, Celebrities of the Arab and Islamic Worlds) (Cairo: Muassassat ar-Rissala, 1972), vol. 5, p. 197.

25. Jack Flam, *Matisse on Art* (Berkeley: University of California Press, 1995), p. 178.

# 13

# Size 6: The Western Women's Harem

It was during my unsuccessful attempt to buy a cotton skirt in an American department store that I was told my hips were too large to fit into a size 6. That distressing experience made me realize how the image of beauty in the West can hurt and humiliate a woman as much as the veil does when enforced by the state police in extremist nations such as Iran, Afghanistan, or Saudi Arabia. Yes, that day I stumbled onto one of the keys to the enigma of passive beauty in Western harem fantasies. The elegant saleslady in the American store looked at me without moving from her desk and said that she had no skirt my size. "In this whole big store, there is no skirt for me?" I said. "You are joking." I felt very suspicious and thought that she just might be too tired to help me. I could understand that. But then the saleswoman added a condescending judgment, which sounded to me like an Imam's *fatwa*. It left no room for discussion:

"You are too big!" she said.

"I am too big compared to what?" I asked, looking at her intently, because I realized that I was facing a critical cultural gap here.

"Compared to a size 6," came the saleslady's reply.

Her voice had a clear-cut edge to it that is typical of those who enforce religious laws. "Size 4 and 6 are the norm," she went on, encouraged by my bewildered look. "Deviant sizes such as the one you need can be bought in special stores."

That was the first time that I had ever heard such non-sense about my size. In the Moroccan streets, men's flattering comments regarding my particularly generous hips have for decades led me to believe that the entire planet shared their convictions. It is true that with advancing age, I have been hearing fewer and fewer flattering comments when walking in the medina, and sometimes the silence around me in the bazaars is deafening. But since my face has never met with the local beauty standards, and I have often had to defend myself against remarks such as *zirafa* (giraffe), because of my long neck, I learned long ago not to rely too much on the outside world for my sense of self-worth. In fact, paradoxically, as I discovered when I went to Rabat as a student, it was the self-reliance that I had developed to protect myself against "beauty blackmail" that made me attractive to others. My male fellow students could not believe that I did not give a damn about what they thought about my body. "You know, my dear," I would say in response to one of them, "all I need to survive is bread, olives, and sardines. That you think my neck is too long is your problem, not mine."

In any case, when it comes to beauty and compliments, nothing is too serious or definite in the medina, where everything can be negotiated. But things seemed to be different in that American department store. In fact, I have to confess that I lost my usual self-confidence in that New York environment. Not that I am always sure of myself, but I don't walk around the Moroccan streets or down the university corridors wondering what people are thinking about me. Of course, when I hear a compliment, my ego expands like a cheese soufflé, but on the whole, I don't expect to hear much from others. Some mornings, I feel ugly because I am sick or tired; others, I feel wonderful because it is sunny out or I have written a good paragraph. But suddenly, in that peaceful American store that I had entered so triumphantly, as a sovereign consumer ready to spend money, I felt savagely attacked. My hips, until then the sign of a relaxed and uninhibited maturity, were suddenly being condemned as a deformity.

"And who decides the norm?" I asked the saleslady, in an attempt to regain some self-confidence by challenging the established rules. I never let others evaluate me, if only because I remember my childhood too well. In ancient Fez, which valued round-faced plump adolescents, I was repeatedly told that I was too tall, too skinny, my cheekbones were too high, my eyes were too slanted. My mother often complained that I would never find a husband and urged me to study and learn all that I could, from storytelling to embroidery, in order to survive. But I often retorted that since "Allah had created me the way I am, how could he be so wrong, Mother?" That would silence the poor woman for a while, because if she contradicted me, she would be attacking God himself. And this tactic of glorifying my strange looks as a divine gift not only helped me to survive in my stuffy city, but also caused me to start believing the story myself. I became almost self-confident. I say almost, because I realized early on that self-confidence is not a tangible and stable thing like a silver bracelet that never changes over the years. Self-confidence is like a tiny fragile light, which goes off and on. You have to replenish it constantly.

"And who says that everyone must be a size 6?" I joked to the saleslady that day, deliberately neglecting to mention size 4, which is the size of my skinny twelve-year-old niece.

At that point, the saleslady suddenly gave me an anxious look. "The norm is everywhere, my dear," she said. "It's all over, in the magazines, on television, in the ads. You can't escape it. There is Calvin Klein, Ralph Lauren, Gianni Versace, Giorgio Armani, Mario Valentino, Salvatore Ferragamo, Christian Dior, Yves Saint-Laurent, Christian

Lacroix, and Jean-Paul Gaultier. Big department stores go by the norm." She paused and then concluded, "If they sold size 14 or 16, which is probably what you need, they would go bankrupt."

She stopped for a minute and then stared at me, intrigued. "Where on earth do you come from? I am sorry I can't help you. Really, I am." And she looked it too. She seemed, all of a sudden, interested, and brushed off another woman who was seeking her attention with a cutting, "Get someone else to help you, I'm busy." Only then did I notice that she was probably my age, in her late fifties. But unlike me, she had the thin body of an adolescent girl. Her knee-length, navy blue, Chanel dress had a white silk collar reminiscent of the subdued elegance of aristocratic French Catholic schoolgirls at the turn of the century. A pearl-studded belt emphasized the slimness of her waist. With her meticulously styled short hair and sophisticated makeup, she looked half my age at first glance.

"I come from a country where there is no size for women's clothes," I told her. "I buy my own material and the neighborhood seamstress or craftsman makes me the silk or leather skirt I want. They just take my measurements each time I see them. Neither the seamstress nor I know exactly what size my new skirt is. We discover it together in the making. No one cares about my size in Morocco as long as I pay taxes on time. Actually, I don't know what my size is, to tell you the truth."

The saleswoman laughed merrily and said that I should advertise my country as a paradise for stressed working women. "You mean you don't watch your weight?" she inquired, with a tinge of disbelief in her voice. And then, after a brief moment of silence, she added in a lower register, as if talking to herself: "Many women working in highly paid fashion-related jobs could lose their positions if they didn't keep to a strict diet."

Her words sounded so simple, but the threat they implied was so cruel that I realized for the first time that maybe "size 6" is a more violent restriction imposed on women than is the Muslim veil. Quickly I said good-bye so as not to make any more demands on the saleslady's time or involve her in any more unwelcome, confidential exchanges about age-discriminating salary cuts. A surveillance camera was probably watching us both.

Yes, I thought as I wandered off, I have finally found the answer to my harem enigma. Unlike the Muslim man, who uses space to establish male domination by excluding women from the public arena, the Western man manipulates time and light. He declares that in order to be beautiful, a woman must look fourteen years old. If she dares to look fifty, or worse, sixty, she is beyond the pale. By putting the spotlight on the female child and framing her as the ideal of beauty, he condemns the mature woman to invisibility. In fact, the modern Western man enforces Immanuel Kant's nineteenth-century theories: To be beautiful, women have to appear childish and brainless. When a woman looks mature and self-assertive, or allows her hips to expand, she is condemned as ugly. Thus, the walls of the European harem separate youthful beauty from ugly maturity.

These Western attitudes, I thought, are even more dangerous and cunning than the Muslim ones because the weapon used against women is time. Time is less visible, more fluid than space. The Western man uses images and spotlights to freeze female beauty within an idealized childhood, and forces women to perceive aging—that normal unfolding of the years—as a shameful devaluation. "Here I am, transformed into a dinosaur," I caught myself saying aloud as I went up and down the rows of skirts in the store, hoping to prove the saleslady wrong—to no avail. This Western time-defined veil is even crazier than the space-defined one enforced by the Ayatollahs.

The violence embodied in the Western harem is less visible than in the Eastern harem because aging is not attacked directly, but rather masked as an aesthetic choice. Yes, I suddenly felt not only very ugly but also quite useless in that store, where, if you had big hips, you were simply out of the picture. You drifted into the fringes of nothingness. By putting the spotlight on the prepubescent female, the Western man veils the older, more mature woman, wrapping her in shrouds of ugliness. This idea gives me the chills because it tattoos the invisible harem directly onto a woman's skin. Chinese foot-binding worked the same way: Men declared beautiful only those women who had small, childlike feet. Chinese men did not force women to bandage their feet to keep them from developing normally—all they did was to define the beauty ideal. In feudal China, a beautiful woman was the one who voluntarily sacrificed her right to unhindered physical movement by mutilating her own feet, and thereby proving that her main goal in life was to please men. Similarly, in the Western world, I was expected to shrink my hips into a size 6 if I wanted to find a decent skirt tailored for a beautiful woman. We Muslim women have only one month of fasting, Ramadan, but the poor Western woman who diets has to fast twelve months out of the year. *"Quelle horreur,"* I kept repeating to myself, while looking around at the American women shopping. All those my age looked like youthful teenagers.

According to the writer Naomi Wolf, the ideal size for American models decreased sharply in the 1990s. "A generation ago, the average model weighed 8 percent less than the average American woman, whereas today she weighs 23 percent less. . . . The weight of Miss America plummeted, and the average weight of Playboy Playmates dropped from 11 percent below the national average in 1970 to 17 percent below it in eight years."[1] The shrinking of the ideal size, according to Wolf, is one of the primary reasons for anorexia and other health-related problems: "Eating disorders rose exponentially, and a mass of neurosis was promoted that used food and weight to strip women of . . . a sense of control."[2]

Now, at last, the mystery of my Western harem made sense. Framing youth as beauty and condemning maturity is the weapon used against women in the West just as limiting access to public space is the weapon used in the East. The objective remains identical in both cultures: to make women feel unwelcome, inadequate, and ugly.

The power of the Western man resides in dictating what women should wear and how they should look. He controls the whole fashion industry, from cosmetics to underwear. The West, I realized, was the only part of the world where women's fashion is a man's business. In places like Morocco, where you design your own clothes and discuss them with craftsmen and -women, fashion is your own business. Not so in the West. As Naomi Wolf explains in *The Beauty Myth,* men have engineered a prodigious amount of fetish-like, fashion-related paraphernalia: "Powerful industries—the $33-billion-a-year diet industry, the $20-billion cosmetic industry, the $300-million cosmetic surgery industry, and the $7-billion pornography industry—have arisen from the capital made out of unconscious anxieties, and are in turn able, through their influence on mass culture, to use, stimulate, and reinforce the hallucination in a rising economic spiral."[3]

But how does the system function? I wondered. Why do women accept it?

Of all the possible explanations, I like that of the French sociologist, Pierre Bourdieu, the best. In his latest book, *La Domination Masculine,* he proposes something he calls *"la violence symbolique":* "Symbolic violence is a form of power which is hammered directly on the body, and as if by magic, without any apparent physical constraint. But this magic operates only because it activates the codes pounded in the deepest layers of the body."[4] Reading Bourdieu, I had the impression that I finally understood Western man's psyche better. The cosmetic and fashion industries are only the tip of the iceberg, he states, which is why women are so ready to adhere to their dictates. Something else is going on on a far deeper level. Otherwise, why would women belittle themselves spontaneously? Why, argues Bourdieu, would women make their lives more difficult, for example, by preferring men who are taller or older than they are? "The majority of French women wish to have a husband who is older and also, which seems consistent, bigger as far as size is concerned," writes Bourdieu.[5] Caught in the enchanted submission characteristic of the symbolic violence inscribed in the mysterious layers of the flesh, women relinquish what he calls "les signes ordinaires de la hiérarchie sexuelle," the ordinary signs of sexual hierarchy, such as old age and a larger body. By so doing, explains Bourdieu, women spontaneously accept the subservient position. It is this spontaneity Bourdieu describes as magic enchantment.[6]

Once I understood how this magic submission worked, I

became very happy that the conservative Ayatollahs do not know about it yet. If they did, they would readily switch to its sophisticated methods, because they are so much more effective. To deprive me of food is definitely the best way to paralyze my thinking capabilities.

Both Naomi Wolf and Pierre Bourdieu come to the conclusion that insidious "body codes" paralyze Western women's abilities to compete for power, even though access to education and professional opportunities seem wide open, because the rules of the game are so different according to gender. Women enter the power game with so much of their energy deflected to their physical appearance that one hesitates to say the playing field is level. "A cultural fixation on female thinness is not an obsession about female beauty," explains Wolf. It is "an obsession about female obedience. Dieting is the most potent political sedative in women's history; a quietly mad population is a tractable one."[7] Research, she contends, "confirmed what most women know too well—that concern with weight leads to a 'virtual collapse of self-esteem and sense of effectiveness' and that . . . 'prolonged and periodic caloric restriction' resulted in a distinctive personality whose traits are passivity, anxiety, and emotionality."[8] Similarly, Bourdieu, who focuses more on how this myth hammers its inscriptions onto the flesh itself, recognizes that constantly reminding women of their physical appearance destabilizes them emotionally because it reduces them to exhibited objects. "By confining women to the status of symbolical objects to be seen and perceived by the other, masculine domination . . . puts women in a state of constant physical insecurity. . . . They have to strive ceaselessly to be engaging, attractive, and available."[9] Being frozen into the passive position of an object whose very existence depends on the eye of its beholder turns the educated modern Western woman into a harem slave.

"I thank you, Allah, for sparing me the tyranny of the 'size 6 harem,' " I repeatedly said to myself while seated on the Paris-Casablanca flight, on my way back home at last. "I am so happy that the conservative male elite does not know about it. Imagine the fundamentalists switching from the veil to forcing women to fit size 6."

How can you stage a credible political demonstration and shout in the streets that your human rights have been violated when you cannot find the right skirt?

---

1. Naomi Wolf, *The Beauty Myth: How Images of Beauty Are Used Against Women* (New York: Anchor Books, Doubleday, 1992), p. 185.

2. Ibid., p. 11.

3. Ibid., p. 17.

4. Pierre Bourdieu: "La force symbolique est une forme de pouvoir qui s'exerce sur les corps, directement, et comme par magie, en dehors de toute contraine physique, mais cette magie n'opère qu'en s'appuyant sur des dispositions déposées, tel des ressorts, au plus profond des corps." In *La Domination Masculine* (Paris: Editions du Seuil, 1998), op. cit. p. 44.

Here I would like to thank my French editor, Claire Delannoy, who kept me informed of the latest debates on women's issues in Paris by sending me Bourdieu's book and many others. Delannoy has been reading this manuscript since its inception in 1996 (a first version was published in Casablanca by Edition Le Fennec in 1998 as "Êtes-Vous Vacciné Contre le Harem").

5. *La Domination Masculine,* op. cit., p. 41.

6. Bourdieu, op. cit., p. 42.

7. Wolf, op. cit., p. 187.

8. Wolf, quoting research carried out by S. C. Woolly and O. W. Woolly, op. cit., pp. 187–188.

9. Bourdieu, *La Domination Masculine,* p. 73.

# Index

Index

There appears to be a basis for thinking that Muslim women are raised w/ a greater respect for their own intellect & for their sense of equality — & men recognize this — 20, 23, 26, 38